GAY AND LESBIAN WRITERS

Adrienne Rich

GAY AND LESBIAN WRITERS

James Baldwin

Allen Ginsberg

Adrienne Rich

Sappho

Walt Whitman

Oscar Wilde

GAY AND LESBIAN WRITERS

Adrienne Rich

Amy Sickels

Lesléa Newman
Series Editor

CHELSEA HOUSE
PUBLISHERS
A Haights Cross Communications Company ®
Philadelphia

CHELSEA HOUSE PUBLISHERS

VP, NEW PRODUCT DEVELOPMENT Sally Cheney
DIRECTOR OF PRODUCTION Kim Shinners
CREATIVE MANAGER Takeshi Takahashi
MANUFACTURING MANAGER Diann Grasse

Staff for ADRIENNE RICH

EXECUTIVE EDITOR: Matt Uhler
EDITORIAL ASSISTANT: Sarah Sharpless
PHOTO EDITOR: Sarah Bloom
SERIES AND COVER DESIGNER: Takeshi Takahashi
LAYOUT: EJB Publishing Services

A Haights Cross Communications ✦ Company ®

http://www.chelseahouse.com

First Printing

9 8 7 6 5 4 3 2 1

Library of Congress Cataloging-in-Publication Data

Sickels, Amy.
  Adrienne Rich / Amy Sickels.
    p. cm. — (Gay and lesbian writers)
  "Works by Adrienne Rich": p.
  Includes bibliographical references.
  ISBN 0-7910-8223-7 (alk. paper)
  1. Rich, Adrienne Cecile. 2. Homosexuality and literature—United States—
History—20th century. 3. Poets, American—20th century—Biography. 4.
Lesbians—United States—Biography. I. Title. II. Series.
  PS3535.I233Z88 2005
  811'.54—dc22

                          2004029827

TABLE OF CONTENTS

PRIDE

MANY YEARS AGO, IN 1970 to be exact, I began my career as a high school student. Those were the dark ages, before cell phones and CD players, before computers and cable TV, before the words "gay" and "pride" ever—at least to my knowledge—appeared in the same sentence. In fact, I remember the very first time I saw the word "gay" appear in a newspaper. It was in the early 1970s, a year after the 1969 Stonewall riots when a group of butches and drag queens fought back against a police raid on a gay bar, sparking what was then known as the "gay liberation movement." I was sitting in our Long Island living room with my brothers, my parents, and some visiting relatives. One of the adults picked up the newspaper, read a headline about the anniversary of Stonewall and said in a voice dripping with disapproval, "Well, all I can say is *gay* certainly meant something different in my time." There were a few murmurs of agreement, and then the matter was dropped. I learned very quickly that this subject was taboo in the Newman household.

Not that I had any inkling that I would grow up to be a lesbian. All I knew was that I didn't want to get married and have children, I wasn't interested in boys, and all I wanted to do was read books, write poetry, and spend time with my best friend, Vicki, who lived three houses away. My friendship with Vicki was strictly platonic, but even so, taunts of "Leslie the lezzie, Leslie the lezzie" followed me up and down the hallways of

Jericho High School. (I changed my name from Leslie to Lesléa when I was sixteen largely because, due to my gender-free name, I was, much to my horror, enrolled in the boys' gym class.)

Interestingly enough, Vicki was never once teased for being a lesbian; did my classmates know something I didn't know?

In 1973 I left home to attend the University of Vermont. There was no gay/straight alliance on campus, nor were there courses in gay literature or gay history. Though I studied the poetry of Gertrude Stein, I was never led to believe that Alice B. Toklas was anything more than the poet's housekeeper and cook. Though I studied Walt Whitman's work and read the novels of James Baldwin, there was never any mention of either man's sexuality. And even though I still was unaware of my own sexuality, I knew somehow that I was "different." I did not want the same things most of the young women around me wanted, namely a husband and children. I did not know being a lesbian was a possibility. Since I wasn't interested in boys "that way," I simply thought I was not a sexual being.

What saved me was the Beat movement, and specifically the Beat poets: Allen Ginsberg, Peter Orlovsky, Gary Snyder, Anne Waldman, and Ted Berrigan, all of whom became my teachers when I hitchhiked out to Boulder, Colorado, and enrolled in Naropa Institute's Jack Kerouac School of Disembodied Poetics. The Beats were unabashedly sexual. Allen and Peter were clearly a couple; there was also a pair of lesbians on the faculty who made no secret of the fact that they lived together. I learned about Sappho and the island of Lesbos; I learned that Virginia Woolf and Vita Sackville-West were not merely pen pals; I learned that Emily Dickinson had a correspondence with her sister-in-law Susan Huntington Dickinson that some inter-preted as romantic. And though these women may or may not have been lesbians, the discovery that women could be primary in each other's lives in a passionate way filled me with a sense of excitement and hope. Finally I realized that I wasn't a freak. There were others like me. A world of possibilities opened up before my eyes.

In 1999, I was invited back to my alma mater to be inducted into the Jericho High School Hall of Fame. The world had changed in many ways since I graduated in 1973. The words "gay" and "lesbian" now appeared in many newspapers across the country on a regular basis, and the gay, lesbian, bisexual, and transgendered community even had its own newspapers and magazines. In 1977, Harvey Milk, the first openly out politician in this country, had been elected as a San Francisco City Supervisor (tragically he was assasinated in his office the following year). Most large cities had gay and lesbian pride parades during the month of June and many high schools had gay straight alliances (Concord High School in Concord, Massachusetts started the first GSA in 1989). The "gayby boom" had begun as more and more lesbians and gay men were starting families, and the gay marriage movement was going strong.

Since graduating from high school, my life had changed dramatically as well. In 1988 I met the woman of my dreams and a year later, on September 10, 1989, we celebrated our relationship with a lifetime commitment ceremony (On September 10, 2004, we renewed our vows before a justice of the peace, making our fifteen-year marriage legal in the state of Massachusetts). I had published close to thirty books, most of which had gay or lesbian content, including the picture book, *Heather Has Two Mommies*, which became one of the most controversial and challenged books of the 1990s. And I had become a political activist, speaking out for the rights of lesbians and gay men every chance I could.

When I was inducted into Jericho High School's Hall of Fame, I was invited to come to campus to give a speech at a school assembly. It was only upon arrival that I was informed that the students knew only one thing about me: I was an author. They did not know the titles of my books and they did not know I was a lesbian. Consequently, I had the unexpected opportunity to come out to an entire high school population. If the students were surprised, they did not show it. Jericho students are nothing if not polite. But they did ask interesting questions. They wanted to know if I had dated boys when I was in high school (yes); they wanted to know how old I was when I came out (twenty-seven); they wanted to know if I wished that I were straight (no, but sometimes I wish my hair was). At one point the questions came to a halt, so I decided to ask my audience, "What is it like for gay and lesbian students today at Jericho High School?" The auditorium was quiet for a moment and then a boy called out, "We don't have any gay students."

About a year later, I received an email from a Jericho High School alumna who graduated in June of 1999. She told me she was a lesbian and had known so since she was fifteen years old. She had been at my induction assembly, but did not feel comfortable coming out in front of her peers that day, or even privately to me. Only after she graduated from high school and went away to college did she feel safe enough to be out. Clearly many things had changed since I'd attended Jericho High School and many things had not.

A book is a powerful thing, and literature can change people's lives. If I had read a biography about a lesbian writer when I was in high school, I truly believe my life would have been vastly different. I might very well have been spared years of pain and confusion because I would have known that a life very much like the one I am now living is possible. If the books in this series had been on the Jericho High School curriculum in 1999, perhaps the young woman who sent me an email would have felt safe enough to come out of the closet before graduation.

It is my hope that this book and others like it will help high school students know that not everyone is heterosexual, and that gay, lesbian, bisexual, and transgendered people can and do live happy, productive, inspiring, and creative lives. The writers included in this series have certainly left their mark on society with their award-winning works of poetry and prose. May they inspire us all to be exactly who we are with pride and celebration.

—Lesléa Newman, 2004

A RICH LIFE

ADRIENNE RICH CHANGED MY LIFE. What's more, she did so with just two words: "compulsory" and "heterosexuality." These two words were emblazoned on the front of a pamphlet I came across in 1983. In those days, the feminist print movement was booming. Feminist presses were publishing books by women that mainstream presses found too risky and revolutionary, and feminist bookstores were selling them. Like many women during that time, I was questioning everything, including my sexuality. Luckily I lived in a city that boasted a lesbian/feminist bookstore. I walked into Womonfyre in Northampton, Massachusetts, and immediately felt at home. Crystals refracting rainbows were hanging from the windows; clay goddess figurines stood guard in the glass case in front of the cash register. Smoke from patchouli incense gently wafted through the store, and Alix Dobkin's record "Lavender Jane Loves Women" played on the stereo. And books, newspapers, and magazines were everywhere, many of them locally produced and loosely held together with staples or saddle stitches.

I don't know what drew me to the thin pamphlet that contained Rich's essay, "Compulsory Heterosexuality and Lesbian Existence." Being an avid novel-reader, I imagine I was on my way to the bookstore's fiction section. But I was stopped cold by those two words, which were printed in larger type than the rest of her title, and seemed to leap right off the page. *Compulsory Heterosexuality*. I knew what compulsory meant, having taken compulsory or required exams in both high school and college. And of course I knew what heterosexuality meant—who didn't? But the notion that heterosexuality, the sexual feeling or behavior toward a person of the opposite sex was required, sent my mind reeling. Required by whom? Why was it required? When did it start being required? And most important of all, what about those who ignored such a requirement?

Rich's courageous, intelligent essay was written in 1980 and appears in her book, *Blood, Bread, and Poetry: Selected Prose 1979–1985*. It puts forth the theory of a "lesbian continuum" and explores what Rich calls "women's choice of women as passionate comrades." Rich tears apart the assumption that "most women are innately heterosexual" and validates lesbian existence. Furthermore, she expands that definition to include women who are primary in each other's lives, but not necessarily sexual partners. Upon reading her essay, I realized that I had been a lesbian all my life. Even though I had yet to have a physically intimate relationship with another woman, all my important friendships and emotional relationships were with females, and had been ever since I could remember.

Shortly after my first foray into Womonfyre, I named and claimed my own lesbian identity. At the same time, I was in the process of taking back my Jewish identity, which I had rejected in my early teens. Somehow coming out as a lesbian, which meant being who I fully was as opposed to pretending to be someone I wasn't—a straight girl—brought me back to my Judaism as well.

Back to Womonfyre I went, this time to purchase a book called *Nice Jewish Girls: A Lesbian Anthology* edited by Evelyn Torton Beck. And whose brilliant, powerful, and soul-searching words did I find between the covers? Adrienne Rich's, of course.

Her essay, "Split at the Root," spoke to me even though unlike Rich, my Jewish heritage comes from both sides of my family (Rich's father is Jewish; her mother is not). Still, Rich's feelings of ambivalence about her Jewish heritage matched my own and I found myself asking some of the same questions Rich asks. What does it mean to be a Jewish lesbian? How has anti-Semitism (both external and internal) affected my life? How can I reconcile the patriarchal aspects of Judaism with my feminist values? For me, Rich's essay, like so much of Jewish literature, raised more questions than it answered, and challenged me to think long and hard about my Jewish self, the (mostly) non-Jewish world in which I live, and the relationship between the two.

After reading these two essays, I became curious about Adrienne Rich's poems. And being a newly out lesbian, naturally I was thinking about (read: obsessed with) love. And so I turned to "Twenty-one Love Poems" found in *The Dream of a Common Language*. Rich's gorgeous, sensual poetry kept me company on many a night when I longed to be in another woman's arms. Her poetry assured me that love between women was possible, and what's more, it was well worth waiting for:

> "Did I ever walk the morning streets at twenty,
> my limbs streaming with a purer joy?
> did I lean from any window over the city
> listening for the future
> as I listen here with nerves tuned for your ring?"
> (from "Twenty-one Love Poems," section III)

What I particularly admire in Rich's poetry is how the political and the personal intersect. The events described in "Twenty-one Love Poems" do not occur without a context; the

two female lovers live in a world of violence and potential violence. The sixth poem in the series begins with a description of
the hands of the narrator's beloved:

Your small hands, precisely equal to my own—
only the thumb is larger, longer—in these hands
I could trust the world ...

And the poem ends:

such hands might carry out an unavoidable violence
with such restraint, with such a grasp
of the range and limits of violence
that violence ever after would be obsolete.
(from "Twenty-one Love Poems" section VI)

Amy Sickels' fine biography of Adrienne Rich illuminates
the life of the writer and a rich life it is indeed. A former
teacher of mine once said, "Your life is the poem," and of all the
poets I know, Adrienne Rich proves that to be true. She lives by
her words which are honest, challenging, brave, and beautiful.
She takes nothing for granted, questions everything, and never
plays it safe for fear of conflict or controversy. Her life and her
words dare us to dream big and work to change the world into
a better place for all living beings. A world free of sexism,
racism, classism, anti-Semitism, ageism, and homophobia.
Such a world may never exist, but that is almost irrelevant.
What matters is working toward that goal with our thoughts,
action, and speech. We are fortunate to have Adrienne Rich as a
role model to show us the way.

one

Transformation

I was writing very little, partly from fatigue, that female fatigue of suppressed anger and loss of contact with my own being; partly from the discontinuity of female life with its attention to small chores, errands, work that others constantly undo, small children's constant needs. What I did write was unconvincing to me; my anger and frustration were hard to acknowledge in or out of poems because in fact I cared a great deal about my husband and children.

—Adrienne Rich, "When We Dead Awaken"

BY THE TIME ADRIENNE RICH was thirty years old, she had given birth to three sons and had published two books of poetry. She had always assumed that she could be both a poet and a mother at once; however, in the 1950s, when her children were young, she nearly gave up writing. For eight years, she disappeared from the literary world.

Then, in 1966, she suddenly broke her silence with the publication of *Snapshots-of-a-Daughter-in-Law*. This book of poems was the first foreshadowing of what would become Adrienne Rich's dramatic transformation from a housewife to a radical lesbian-feminist.

Like many women of the 1950s, Rich was unsatisfied with her life, and felt that marriage and motherhood had taken away her independence. What she wanted most was uninterrupted time; however, her time was taken up by household chores, caring for her children, and supporting her husband in his burgeoning career. "I wanted, then, more than anything, the one of which there was never enough: time to think, time to write," she admitted (Rich, *On Lies, Secrets, and Silence* 44). She felt confused about her vacillating emotions toward her children, and worried that she was a horrendous mother for feeling sparks of resentment and anger. In the early years of motherhood, Rich fell into fits of depression and despondency. She did not have anyone with whom to discuss her growing sense of alienation and melancholy, and it was only in her journal where she could try to make sense of what she was feeling.

After graduating from college, with one book already published, Rich had assumed she would continue on the path to literary success. However, she also wanted to be married, to have children—a status that seemed like the only fulfilling possibility for a woman during this time, the only model. "Rich's realization that she was not by nature the all-patient, all-submissive, all-nurturing woman she believed she had to be in order to rear her children properly came as a terrible shock and a frightening revelation," the critic/biographer Paula Bennett suggests in her book *My Life as a Loaded Gun* (Bennett 185).

As a young mother, Rich stopped writing except for the personal entries in her journals. Then sometime in the late fifties, she slowly began to return to writing. She wrote down pieces of poems whenever she could find time. It was during a span of two years that she composed "Snapshots of a Daughter-in-Law," a poem that "was jotted in fragments during children's naps, brief hours in a library, or at 3:00 A.M. after rising with a wakeful child" (*On Lies, Secrets, and Silence* 44). For Rich, writing this poem was a major revelation. It liberated her from the confines of motherhood, and also from the traditional, neat poems she had composed in her first two books. For the first time, she was writing in a more personal tone, experimenting with a looser, open style. Most importantly, she was writing truthfully about her experience as a woman.

Snapshots signals the first transformation in Rich's life and in her poetry, but it would not be her last. Adrienne Rich is a poet of motion, whose style and subjects have evolved and transformed over the period of her career. However, one aspect that has not changed over the years is her commitment to women's rights, a theme that first appeared in "Snapshots of a Daughter-in-Law."

Writing this poem symbolized a personal discovery for Rich, offering her glimpses of the independent life she wanted to live, and bringing her closer to what would become the primary source of her poetry, that blend of personal and political. In *Adrienne Rich's Poetry and Prose*, the critic Albert Gelpi, a long-time admirer of Rich's work, emphasizes how monumental this book was for the future of Rich's poetry:

Snapshots of a Daughter-in-Law (1963) is the transitional

book in Adrienne Rich's development. Eight years had inter-
vened between volumes, and they were years of great change,
so that the book begins in one place and ends in another.
What happens is the crucial event in the career of any artist:
a penetration into experience which makes for a distin-
guishing style. Her themes—the burden of history, the
separateness of individuals, the need for relationship where
there is no other transcendence—begin to find their clari-
fying focus and center: what she is as woman and poet in
late-twentieth-century America. (Rich, et al., *Adrienne Rich's
Poetry and Prose* 285)

Not long after the publication of *Snapshots*, Rich became
active in the Civil Rights movement, which then led to her
deep involvement in the Women's Liberation Movement. The
Women's Movement radically changed Rich, both in terms of
her political convictions and her poetry. She committed herself
to fighting for the rights of women, and for ending exploitation
and suffering. Being a part of a community of women also
encouraged her to finally be honest about her sexuality. When
she was forty-six years old, Adrienne Rich came out of the
closet, and since then she has lived her life openly as a lesbian.

The publication of *Snapshots of a Daughter-in-Law* hinted
that Adrienne Rich was no longer content to live a life of
silence or invisibility, and that she had committed herself to
speaking out. Since then, she has adhered to this principle, in
both her poetry and her political activism. Her life has been a
remarkable journey, filled with struggles and revelations.
Although her audience may recognize her now as an accomplished poet and political force, there was of course a time
when it was not this way. "The experience of motherhood,"
Rich wrote in 1982, "was eventually to radicalize me."

two

A Father's Ambition

where the father walks up and down
telling the child to work, work
harder than anyone has worked before?
                    —Adrienne Rich, "Sources"

ADRIENNE CECILE RICH WAS BORN on May 16, 1929, to Arnold and Helen Jones Rich in Baltimore, Maryland. The daughter of a Jewish father and a Christian mother, Rich came of age during the difficult years of the Great Depression and World War II in a financially secure, highly educated, and artistically inclined household. The neighborhood the Riches lived in was white, middle-class, and Protestant, and the family was sheltered from the economic struggles many other Americans faced. Although Rich sometimes felt that she did not fit in with her surroundings, feeling "split at the root" early on in her life, there was nothing about Adrienne Rich's upbringing to suggest that this precocious, obedient girl would turn into a prominent lesbian-feminist who would spend her life fighting social injustices, including homophobia, sexism, racism, and poverty.

Adrienne Rich's parents valued art and literature over politics or social concerns, and they filled their home with books and music. Both of her parents, who were Southerners, came from families who worked hard to make sure their children were well educated and successful. Adrienne's father, Arnold, had grown up in Birmingham, Alabama. Arnold's father, Samuel Rich, was an Ashkenazic Jew (descended from central/eastern Europe, Poland, and Russia) who had immigrated from Austria-Hungary, and his mother, Hattie Rice, whose family had been Sephardic Jews (descended from Spain, Portugal, North Africa, and the Middle East), came from Vicksburg, Mississippi. Samuel Rich had owned a successful shoe store, which allowed his family to live fairly prosperously.

Arnold's parents believed in the value of education and the promise of the American dream, and they instilled these ideas in their son. When he was a young man, Arnold attended the Bingham military school in North Carolina, and after graduation he studied at the University of Virginia. In 1915, Arnold went to study at Johns Hopkins Medical School.

When he was twenty-two years old, Arnold met Helen Jones, a pianist and composer who descended from a southern white Protestant family. Rich's mother's family owned land, but they were not considered wealthy. Like Arnold's family, Helen's family also valued education. Helen's mother had attended a convent school, the best education a woman could receive at the time, and her father made a living as a successful tobacco salesman.

Helen trained seriously for years as a concert pianist and composer, winning a scholarship to study with the director at the prestigious Peabody Conservatory in Baltimore. An independent and ambitious woman, she also spent time teaching at a private girls' school to earn her way to study in New York, Paris, and Vienna. Although Helen had many male admirers, at this time she focused solely on her musical career. "From the age of sixteen, she had been a young belle," Rich wrote about her mother, "who could have married at any time, but she also possessed unusual talent, determination, and independence for her time and place" (Rich, *Of Woman Born* 221).

When Helen met Arnold, she was charmed by his intellectual vigor and ambition. The two were engaged for ten years, during which time Helen continued to perform concerts and study music, and Arnold finished his medical training and began to establish himself in academic medicine. They married in 1925 and moved to Baltimore for Arnold's work in the Department of Pathology at Johns Hopkins Medical School, where Arnold, who made many contributions to the field, would eventually become an esteemed professor of pathology. After they were married, Helen gave up her promising career as a concert pianist in order to care for her daughters and support her husband's professional success, a sacrifice that Adrienne did not question until years later when she found herself rigorously re-examining the meaning of marriage and motherhood.

> My father ... assumed that [my mother] would give her life
> over to the enhancement of his. She would manage his
> household with the formality and grace becoming to a med-
> ical professor's wife, though on a limited budget; she would
> 'keep up' her music, though there was no question of letting
> her composing and practice conflict with her duties as a wife
> and mother. (*Of Woman Born* 221)

Both Rich's mother and her maternal grandmother had been
resigned to live their lives as "frustrated artists and intellectuals,
a lost writer and a lost composer between them" (Rich, *Blood,
Bread, and Poetry* 102). Rich speculated that if her maternal
grandmother Mary Gravely, who loved books and avidly wrote
in a journal, had lived in a different era, she too would have
pursued a literary career.

When Adrienne was a child, her mother taught her to play
the piano. "For years we battled over music lessons," Rich wrote
in "Solfeggietto," but it was not until she was older that Rich
considered her mother's passion for music. Rich later regretted
that during the lessons, she had not asked "what that keyboard
meant to you/the hours of solitude the practising/your life of
prize-recitals lifted hopes."

Along with the piano lessons, Helen tried to instill the manners of a southern lady into her daughters and also helped
educate them—a responsibility shared and initiated by Adrienne's father. Both Adrienne and her younger sister Cynthia
were educated at home until the fourth grade, an experience
which provided them with intellectual prowess, but also isolated them from other children their age. Arnold insisted that
the family should strive to be exceptional: "[T]he message I got
was that we were really superior: nobody else's father had collected so many books, had traveled so far, knew so many
languages" (*Blood, Bread, and Poetry* 113). Arnold put a

tremendous amount of pressure on his daughters, especially Adrienne, whom he often treated as a son. He wanted to transform his daughters, for Adrienne to become a poet and Cynthia to become a novelist.

Arnold Rich was an intellectually curious and artistic man, "brilliant, ambitious, possessed by his own drive," who had a genuine reverence for education and learning (*Of Woman Born* 221). He read voraciously, played the violin and composed music, and devoted himself to educating his children. Arnold was extremely well read, possessing a great love for poetry, especially for the pre-Raphaelites and the Victorians. His library included the works of Lord Alfred Tennyson, John Keats, Matthew Arnold, William Blake, Dante Gabriel Rossetti, Charles Swinburne, and Thomas Carlyle, all of which were early influences on Rich. The positive impact he had on Adrienne's intellect, poetic sensibility, and work ethic is undeniable; yet, at the same time, he was so querulous and ruthless in his demands that even as an adult, Rich felt she could not escape his authority.

Although Helen supervised many of the school lessons, it was Arnold who reigned over Adrienne's education. He closely examined all of her schoolwork, measuring everything she did against his impossibly high standards and challenging her to surpass these goals. He gave her books on poetry, and at five years old, at her father's request, Rich was copying lines of poetry, such as "The Tyger" by William Blake, into a ruled notebook as handwriting exercises. Under her father's guided supervision, she began writing her own poems. Arnold taught Adrienne the craft of poetry, gave her books on poetic rhyme, meter, and form, and read and critiqued all of her poems. "I was supposed to write something every day and show it to him," Rich told an interviewer decades later. "At some points I hated that. But it was probably a good thing" (O'Mahoney).

For much of her life, Rich felt torn about her father's influence on her education; while she was grateful that he introduced her to poetry and instilled in her a strong work ethic, she resented his controlling methods. "[My father's] investment in my intellect and talent was egotistical, tyrannical, opinionated, and terribly wearing," she wrote in "Split at the Root." "He taught me, nevertheless, to believe in hard work, to mistrust easy inspiration, to write and rewrite; to feel that I was a person of the book, even though a woman; to take ideas seriously. He made me feel, at a very young age, the power of language and that I could share in it" (*Adrienne Rich's Poetry and Prose* 232).

Although she mostly wrote to please her father, Rich also felt a personal connection to poetry early on in life. She felt a natural kinship with the genre, and as a child, already suspected that poetry was "more than music and images; it was also revelation, information, a kind of teaching" (*Blood, Bread, and Poetry* 169). She soon realized that poetry could teach her how to live:

> I thought it could offer clues, intimations, keys to questions that already stalked me, questions I could not even frame yet: *What is possible in this life? What does "love" mean, this thing that is so important? What is this other thing called "freedom" or "liberty"—is it like love, a feeling? What have human beings lived and suffered in the past? How am I going to live my life?* (169)

Even as a child, poetry symbolized a powerful vehicle for Rich, a way for her to express herself, a window by which she could examine, but not retreat from, the world. "[F]rom a very young age poetry was always a sustenance for me," she explained. "It was a way of going deeper into things, it was never escapism. It was a way, as a very young child, of finding out about life" (Moyers 347).

Adrienne Rich was a small, frail girl with dark eyes and hair. She was highly nervous and tense, and at a young age, she began to develop facial tics, which she believed were the result of her father's tyrannical behavior. Arnold could often be punitive if Adrienne did not obey. Once when she was four years old, he locked her in a closet for misbehaving, and although she screamed and cried, she was not allowed to come out until she was quiet. She often showed her temper, a "little girl, round-faced with/clenched fists." Despite her occasional outbursts, for the most part Adrienne was a serious, hard-working child, who wanted to impress her father and "tried for a long time to please him, or rather, not to displease him" (*Blood, Bread, and Poetry* 38). Rich's most autobiographical writing has focused on her relationship with her father and her conflicted feelings about the influence he had on her childhood.

One ongoing conflict Rich had with her father was that she felt he raised her to be in unconscious denial of her religious and cultural heritage, a topic she examines in the essay "Split at the Root: An Essay on Jewish Identity." Arnold Rich was a short man with slender build, dark wiry hair, deep set eyes, and a high brow, and he looked, according to Rich, "recognizably Jewish"; however, he rarely referred to himself as Jewish (*Blood, Bread, and Poetry* 102). Her father's ambivalence toward his Jewish heritage contributed to Adrienne's feelings of isolation and separateness, which grew stronger as she entered adolescence. She recalls in "Split" one year when she was participating in a school production of Shakespeare's *The Merchant of Venice*, and her father, while helping her rehearse her lines, instructed her to say the word "Jew" with more scorn and contempt in her voice. It was a memory that, from Rich's point of view, exemplified her father's shame about his Jewish-ness (*Blood, Bread, and Poetry* 104).

Although neither of her parents were religious or attended church, Adrienne and her sister were baptized and sent to an Episcopal church, which Adrienne attended for five years "without belief" (*Blood, Bread, and Poetry* 105). The required church attendance seemed to be mainly a social pretense. Helen wanted her daughters to fit in with the other children. She reasoned that claiming to be Episcopalian was better than to not claim any religion at all, and certainly safer than claiming to be Jewish. Ironically, when Adrienne came home from church, her father read to her Thomas Paine's diatribe against institutional religion, *The Age of Reason* (1794), as a way to counter what she had just been taught at Sunday School.

The deep undercurrent of anti-Semitism in America likely encouraged Arnold and Helen to raise their children as Protestants. Rich was born on the verge of the Great Depression in a city that was predominately Protestant, as well as deeply segregated and racially divided. Although Rich was aware early on of the racism, she said years later in an interview with David Montenegro, "That kind of thing a child grows up acutely aware of, even if it's never talked about, and of course, there was a great deal of pressure not to talk about it" (*Adrienne Rich's Poetry and Prose* 262). In her parents' tightly woven social world, racism, as well as anti-Semitism, was never mentioned, and most people pretended neither existed.

As a result of her parents' indifference toward religion, Adrienne did not know anything about the Jewish religion, and she would not even enter a synagogue until she left Baltimore as a young adult. Rich later theorized that her father had feared that others, such as his co-workers or neighbors, would stereotype them as being pushy, loud, greedy, or the "wrong kind" of Jew (*Blood, Bread, and Poetry* 114). To counter those stereotypical images, Arnold carefully raised his daughters to speak quietly, to be demure and modest, "to assimilate with a world which might see us as too flamboyant" (111). Arnold's mother, who lived with the Riches from time to time, set an example for her granddaughters. Rich recalled her paternal grandmother as being "a model of circumspect behavior" and "ladylike to an extreme" (111). Rich later realized how her father's desire to protect the family from others' possible prejudices contributed to the stifling atmosphere of their home: "The Riches were proud, but we also had to be very careful. Our behavior had to be more impeccable than other people's. Strangers were not to be trusted, nor even friends; family issues must never go beyond the family" (113).

Although much of Rich's childhood centered around trying to win her father's approval, she also pursued her own childlike interests. She enjoyed playing with paper dolls and listening to the radio. She was a fan of the child star Shirley Temple, and when Temple published a letter in the national newspapers about eating vegetables, Rich was delighted: "I was impressed by Shirley Temple as a little girl my age who had power: she could write a piece for the newspapers and have it printed in her own handwriting" (Rich, *What is Found There* 185). Rich also loved to read, exploring many of the books in her father's library and treasuring the moments when she was alone: "The best times were times I was ignored, could talk stories under my breath, loving my impoverished world almost as much as I loved reading" (184).

When Rich was nine years old, her homeschooling ended, and she was sent to Roland Park Country School, a private girls' school in Baltimore. This change allowed her a brief reprieve from her father's control: "Mercifully, at last, I was sent to school, to discover other real children, born into other families, other kinds of lives. Not a wide range, at a private school for white girls. Still, a new horizon" (*What Is Found There* 187). Although attending school expanded Rich's social world, she still often felt apart from the other girls, as if she didn't belong.

In 1939, a year after Adrienne began attending school, the World's Fair came to New York, and the Rich family took the train from Baltimore to attend the event. Ten-year-old Adrienne kept a "Line-A-Day" diary, in which she poignantly observed: "The greatest part was the World of Tomorrow. Men and women of Tomorrow appeared in the sky and sang" (*What Is Found There* 186). The futuristic world, to her young eyes, seemed full of hope and good fortune. Little did she know that momentous national and international events were unfolding across the globe. One month after the World's Fair, during a time when Americans were experiencing the end of the Great Depression, war was declared in Europe. Soon Adrienne's childhood experiences would include blackouts and air-raids at school. However, despite the outbreak of World War II, Rich's life, like the lives of the majority of American children, for the most part was unaffected.

Adolescence, however, proved to be a confusing period in Adrienne's life. Although Adrienne was happy to be attending school and to not be spending all of her time with her parents, she was not a popular student, nor did she participate in many social activities. She tended to feel isolated and uncertain about how she was supposed to act. Many of the other girls were dating, and much of their talk centered around relationships and boyfriends. Adrienne did not go out on any dates, and she also didn't think about boys the way the other girls did. She was decidedly more interested in writing poetry. "[F]rom the age of thirteen or fourteen, I had felt I was only acting the part of a feminine creature. At the age of sixteen my fingers were almost constantly ink-stained" (*Of Woman Born* 25).

It is not exactly clear when Rich began to realize she was

attracted to other women. She perhaps felt "different" as a teenager which contributed to her loneliness, but it was not until adulthood that her lesbian desires would become apparent to her. America in the 1940s did not allow for sexual differences, and for a young girl growing up in a middle-class neighborhood in Baltimore, Maryland, there would have been virtually no exposure to gays or lesbians,

1930s–1950s Lesbian History

In the 1930s, lesbianism was well hidden and ignored on all social levels. Lesbians were considered monstrosities, and most women were unwilling to proclaim their love for other women, since medical doctors of the 1930s were determined to prevent homosexuality through treatments that went largely unchallenged.

The change of the 1940s, when men were being sent off to war and female labor became vital to the country, had a profound affect on lesbian visibility. Although still discreet, lesbians in general felt freer to seek each other out. The absence of men on the home front, and the fact that many women were now economically independent, made it easier to socialize with each other. However, by the time the war ended and the men had returned, lesbianism was again considered an illness. If a woman proclaimed herself a lesbian, she risked losing her job and family, and she could even be committed as borderline psychotic.

Despite the McCarthy witch-hunts of lesbians and gays, in which many lives were ruined, the 1950s was a pivotal time for emerging lesbian politics. Several groups formed, including the predominately male Mattachine Society in 1951, and the all-lesbian Daughters of Bilitis in 1955, which focused on educating the public that lesbians and gays were no different from other people. The 1950s marks the beginning of the gay and lesbian activism that would resurface in the 1970s.

unless they were presented as sick, deviant, or perverted; the possibility that Rich could be a lesbian most likely did not enter her realm of conscious thought during this time. There was certainly nothing in the books on her father's shelves that could speak to her about the love between women. Many years later, looking back on adolescence, Rich realized that she had feelings for women early on, but had no way to acknowledge these desires to herself. "My history is a very different history from the woman who knew from the age of 12 that she was a dyke," she told Elly Bulkin in 1977. "Women like me were totally in the closet to ourselves and I blame that silence very much" (Bulkin 65).

What did become more apparent to Rich, however, was the isolation she felt in regard to her religious and cultural heritage. When she was fifteen years old, Rich learned of the Holocaust at a movie theater in Baltimore that was showing news reels of the Allied Liberation of the concentration camps. Something inside of her immediately changed on viewing those images. She recalled the immediate devastation and isolation she felt upon viewing the films: "One thing was clear: there was nobody in my world with whom I could discuss those films" (*Blood, Bread, and Poetry* 107). She did not know how to speak to her peers or to her parents about the atrocities in Europe because nobody else seemed to be talking about these horrors, and thus her moment of discovery created another thick layer of isolation and silence. It was not until a few years later, when she left Baltimore at eighteen, that she would begin to actively explore her Jewish heritage.

Being a woman, a Jew, and a lesbian would one day incite Adrienne Rich's politics and activism, but for now she was either unaware of these "differences" or she did not know how to speak of them. Yet each facet of her identity added to her feelings of isolation; she wanted to belong, but usually felt apart, whether at home or at school. She sought out ways to connect herself to the world. Poetry continued to be her primary guide and inspiration during her coming of age; however, often she felt she could not recognize herself in what she read. Years later, in her essay, "When We Dead Awaken," in noting the absence of women in the Western Canon and in history, Rich recalls how she had futilely searched for "*her* way of being in the world, since she too has been putting words and images together; she is looking eagerly for guides, maps, possibilities ... she comes up against something that negates everything she is about: she meets the image of Woman in books written by men" (*On Lies, Secrets, and Silence* 39).

Most of the books in her father's library were predominately written by white male authors. Though these books introduced her to poetry and the beauty of language, they did not offer Rich the possibilities of being. At the time, this world—Baltimore, her family, her father's library—was all that Adrienne Rich had ever known, and although she often felt apart from her surroundings, she did not question this world. It would not be until years later that she would discover other voices outside of the Western Canon, which would help her to better understand herself and inspire her to take bold risks in her poetry, politics, and life.

chapter
three

Searching for Roots

Because what isn't named is often more permeating than what is, I believe my father's Jewishness profoundly shaped my own identity and our family existence.
— Adrienne Rich, "Split at the Root"

IN 1947, WHEN EIGHTEEN-YEAR-OLD Adrienne Rich left Baltimore to attend Radcliffe College, which then was still a women's college, the world suddenly opened up to her. This was a critical move for Rich: not only had she left home, but she had also escaped her father's authority. "It was a great, expanding world," Rich later recalled. "I thought that Cambridge, Massachusetts, was Athens" (O'Mahoney). She instantly felt more comfortable in this liberal, intellectual milieu than she had ever felt in Baltimore, which had always seemed too conservative and conventional. Here she was surrounded by intellectuals, writers, and artists, and for the first time, she found herself among other Jewish women. Rich felt a freedom she had not before experienced. These new friends, who were not ashamed of their Jewish heritage, welcomed Rich and taught her what her parents never had about holidays, foods, and customs. Rich, "flirting with identity," bought a reproduction of a Chagall portrait of a rabbi to hang on her wall (*Blood, Bread, and Poetry* 108). She hoped to figure out where she belonged, to claim a more authentic identity, and she began to look more closely at her Judaism and its noted absence from her parents' lives.

Re-claiming her Jewish roots was not a simple process, and it was something that Rich would return to throughout much of her adult life. Although in college she was meeting and befriending young Jewish women, she still felt pressured to ignore or disclaim her Jewish background. One particular memory that haunted her was a time that she was getting a dress tailored by a seamstress, "a short, dark woman wearing heavy glasses, an accent so foreign I could not understand her words. Something about her presence was very powerful and disturbing to me" (*Blood, Bread, and Poetry* 109). The old woman, in a hurried whisper, asked Rich if she was Jewish, and in a moment of panic, Rich abruptly rejected the woman's hopeful question: "Eighteen years of training in assimilation sprang into the reflex by which I shook my head, rejecting her, and muttered, 'No'" (109). She was afraid that if she said yes, she would be associating herself with the Jewish seamstress and thus undermining the image she had of herself as educated, intellectual, and wholly American: "I saw the frightened immigrant, the seamstress hemming the skirts of college girls, the wandering Jew. But I was an American college girl having her skirt hemmed" (109).

Despite her complicated feelings about her identity, for the most part, while she was in college, Rich felt encouraged to learn more about the Jewish religion. She understood that because her mother was not Jewish that by Jewish law Rich technically could not call herself a Jew; however, this technicality did not dissuade her from wanting to learn more about her family background, to somehow reconcile her father's Jewish heritage with her own Protestant upbringing.

After a year of college, Rich, "flaming with new insights, new information," visited her parents and tried to have a forthright conversation with her father about family ancestry (*Blood, Bread, and Poetry* 110). She had recently read a poem by Karl Shapiro that began, "To hate the Negro and avoid the Jew/is the curriculum" and for the first time, she began to consider the brutal anti-Semitism her father must have faced as a young man. At the time of his daughter's visit, Arnold Rich was waiting to be appointed to the professorship of pathology at Johns Hopkins, and according to Rich, no Jew had ever before held a professional chair at the medical school. Most likely, her father probably felt even more pressure to not draw attention his Jewish heritage. When Adrienne tried to engage her father in the conversation, he told her that she was wrong, that he had never denied that he was Jewish, but that he believed in the values of science, not religion. For Rich, the abrupt conversation re-emphasized how little she knew about her father: "I realized that I never in my whole life knew what my father was really feeling" (*Blood, Bread, and Poetry* 113).

In "Split at the Root" Rich eloquently captures the entanglement of her relationship with her father, which was always one of admiration and contention, and she delineates the way his ambivalence toward his Jewish heritage affected their family existence, which Rich explains was "shaped both by external anti-Semitism and my father's self-hatred, and by his Jewish pride" (*Blood, Bread, and Poetry* 112). Although Rich wished for her father to show more affirmation for his Jewish roots, she also sympathized with his vacillation, considering that he had probably encountered anti-Semitism throughout his life even if he didn't speak of it. Interestingly, Rich was also able to see that her father also felt "Jewish pride," but that he called it something else: "achievement, aspiration, genius, idealism" (112).

Like most young people, Rich was searching for her place in the world, and poetry continued to be a primary outlet for her creativity and a way for her to navigate her way through life. She began to read poets that were not a part of her father's library, seeking out older woman poets such as Sappho, Edna Millay, Emily Dickinson, H.D., and Christina Rossetti. Although these poets provided Rich with a different perspective, perhaps one closer to her own, she still upheld the male poets as being the key mentors for her work. All of Rich's early poetry teachers, beginning with her father and continuing through her college studies, were men. Later, in re-examining her education, Rich felt that even when she was reading women poets at this point in her life, she was still trying to force their work to fit into a male perspective, "looking in them for the same things I had found in the poetry of men, because I wanted women poets to be the equals of men, and to be equal was still confused with sounding the same" (*On Lies, Secrets, and Silence* 39).

During the 1950s, most American universities were blatantly geared toward educating men. For example, Harvard's Lamont Library was off-limits to women because it was feared they would distract male students, and the president of the university saw no reason to increase the number of female undergraduates, since the main goal was to "train leaders." Rich has written about the noticeable absence of women at Harvard and Radcliffe. During her four years at college, she never once had a woman professor. "Women students were simply not taken very seriously," she wrote. "Harvard's message to women was an elite mystification: we were, of course, part of Mankind; we were special, achieving women, or we would not have been there; but of course our real goal was to marry—if possible, a Harvard graduate" (*On Lies, Secrets, and Silence* 238).

Although the literature classes did not provide Rich with works by women authors—those she sought out on her own—they did expose her to more modern poetry, which had not been a part of her father's library: "For all the poetry I grew up with—the Blake, the Keats, the Swinburne and the Shelley, the Elizabeth Barrett Browning, the Whitman, the domesticated versions of Dickinson—in my twenties a greater ocean fell open before me, with its contradictory currents and undertows" (*What is Found There* 190). She began devouring the work of Robert Frost, Dylan Thomas, Wallace Stevens, and especially W.B. Yeats—who interested Rich because of the "dialogue between art and politics" that was combined with "the sound of his language" (*Blood, Bread, and Poetry* 174). The canon of modernist poetry, including T.S. Eliot's "The Waste Land" and Hart Crane's "The Bridge," was important to her development as a poet. "I was exceptionally well grounded in formal technique, and I loved the craft," she explained. "What I was groping for was something larger, a sense of vocation, what it means to live as a poet—not how to write poetry, but wherefore" (*What is Found There* 195).

One person who had a tremendous influence on Rich was one of her Harvard professors, Francis Otto Matthiessen. Matthiessen lectured on five poets—Blake, Keats, Byron, Yeats, and Stevens—and he also spoke about the world beyond Cambridge, Massachusetts. Matthiessen inspired Rich not only for his passion for language and poetry, but also for his fearless devotion to politics and worldly events. This was the late forties and early fifties, and the social and political atmosphere had changed drastically since the years of Rich's childhood. During the thirties and forties, when she had been growing up, the culture was defined by "economic depression, social unrest, war, and also [by] affirmed political art" (*Blood, Bread, and Poetry* 171). Now, during her college years, the country was dominated by the Cold War, fears of Communism and homosexuality, and outspoken anti-Semitism. Matthiessen, a committed socialist and a gay man, spoke of

Debbie Brown

Ruth Seid, publishing under the pseudonym of Jo Sinclair, is often credited with creating the first fully developed lesbian character in the person of Debbie Brown. Though many critics have considered Jake Brown, Debbie's brother, to be the protagonist of Sinclair's first novel, *Wasteland*, Debbie Brown's character remains central to the novel. *Wasteland* deals effectively with, and is often considered a celebration of, ethnicity (Jake struggles with his Jewish identity) and sexual orientation. Though her book won the Harper Prize in 1946 and remained a bestseller, Sinclair would not again make such overt attempts at the subject matter.

political movements with the conviction that they mattered as much as poetry. His teaching approach was highly unusual during this time, as most professors rarely mentioned the world beyond the text. With Matthiessen, however, poetry "never remained in the realm of pure textual criticism" (172).

Rich came from a family that cared for literature and art, not politics, and at this point in her life she "had no political ideas of [her] own" (Rich, *Collected Early Poems* xx). Matthiessen exposed her to other ways of thinking about literature—although she did not realize the significant impact he had made on her life until later. During Rich's sophomore year, Matthiessen committed suicide. He would leave a long-lasting impression on Rich: "That class perhaps affected my life as a poet more than anything else that happened to me in college" (*Blood, Bread, and Poetry* 172).

Several other teachers noticed Rich's poetic talents and encouraged her to enter some of her verses into the 1951 Yale Younger Poets Competition, a prestigious prize awarded for a first book. This year's judge, the renowned poet and influential critic W.H. Auden, chose Rich's book as the winner and also offered to write the preface of her book. Thus, twenty-one-year-old Adrienne Rich, who had just graduated Phi Beta Kappa from Radcliffe, published her first book and entered a society of poets that was almost exclusively male.

In the preface to *A Change of World* (1951), Auden complimented Rich as an intelligent, talented young poet. Although grateful at the time to be noticed by a poet of such stature, now, in retrospect, Rich and other critics have called Auden's tone patronizing and sexist. Auden commends Rich for "display[ing] a modesty not so common at that age, which disclaims any extraordinary vision" (*Adrienne Rich's Poetry and Prose* 278). Rich clearly respects the poetry of her predecessors, he explains approvingly, and makes no attempt to challenge her mentors, citing that her poems "are neatly and modestly dressed, speak quietly but do not mumble, respect their elders but are not cowed by them, and do not tell fibs: that, for a first volume, is a good deal" (279).

Most critics today would agree that the poems in *A Change of World* are tidy, metrical, and quiet. These traditional poems echoed the voices of the major Modernist poets of the early twentieth century, including Auden himself. The poems also exhibit the intellectual rigor which her father had instilled in Rich at a young age. Although Rich had not yet discovered her own poetic voice, the poems were well composed, and many readers felt moved by them. The critic, Helen Vendler, for example, who would criticize much of Rich's later work, wrote, "I read it in almost disbelieving wonder; someone my age was writing down my life" (*Adrienne Rich's Poetry and Prose* 300). Although none of these early poems, which are composed in a formal, detached tone, are political or focused on social events, some of the themes are similar to what Rich would grapple with in later work, including themes of power and submissiveness. The examination of marriage also quietly surfaces in "Aunt Jennifer's Tigers": "The massive weight of Uncle's wedding band/Sits heavily upon Aunt Jennifer's hand."

The following year after the book's publication, Rich won a prestigious Guggenheim Fellowship to study in Oxford for one year. As the critic Paula Bennett points out, winning the Yale Competition and receiving the praise of W.H. Auden helped pave Rich's path for more success, as now "she was stamped and approved by the literary establishment and earned its most sought-after awards" (Bennett 167). After spending an Easter vacation in Florence, Rich decided not to return to Oxford and instead spent the rest of her time traveling through Europe and England. While Rich was traveling overseas, she was inspired by the new sights and foreign lands to write new poems.

Unfortunately, this was also the year in which her rheumatoid arthritis began; the affliction would plague her throughout her life.

To her parents' dismay, Rich married Alfred H. Conrad, an economist at Harvard when she returned to the United States in 1953. They held their wedding at the Hillel House, and neither of Rich's parents attended. According to Rich, her parents felt their daughter was marrying the "wrong kind" of Jew: "My father saw this marriage as my having fallen prey to the Jewish family, eastern European division" (*Blood, Bread, and Poetry* 114). Alfred descended from an orthodox Eastern European family, and Rich's parents disapproved not only of his Jewishness, but also of his lower social class.

Marrying Alfred was the first time Rich overtly rebelled against her father's demands: "Such had been the force of his will in our household that for a long time I felt I would have to pay in some terrible way for having disobeyed him" (*Blood, Bread, and Poetry* 116). Although she loved her husband, a part of her also recognized that she had married him in order to "disconnect from [her] first family" (115). Rich was twenty-three years old when she married Alfred, who was twenty-nine. Marrying so soon after graduation, against her father's opposition, liberated the young Rich. Marriage also seemed like the only viable option for a young woman in the 1950s, when women were "living under a then-unquestioned heterosexual imperative" (115). Rich's marriage to Alfred was as much about gaining social approval as it was about disconnecting from her father.

For several years following the marriage, Rich rarely communicated with either of her parents. Instead, she devoted herself to being a good wife to her husband and becoming a part of his family. Ironically, although Rich's husband came from a family that embraced its Jewish background, Alfred was ambivalent about his ethnic and religious identity, and when he attended Harvard to study economics, he changed his last name from Cohen to Conrad. According to Rich, her husband "was both indissolubly connected to his childhood world and terribly ambivalent about it" (*Blood, Bread, and Poetry* 114).

Alfred's large family celebrated Jewish holidays and customs, and the young Rich was longing "to embrace that family, that new and mysterious Jewish world" (115). Alfred's family presented Rich with a chance to more fully explore her Jewish identity, to become a part of a community and to be connected to an ancient religion. She enjoyed visiting her in-laws at their home in Brooklyn, feeling a sense of belonging and intimacy that she had never experienced with her own family:

> In the big, sunny apartment on Eastern Parkway, the table would be spread on Saturday afternoons with a white or an embroidered cloth and plates of coffeecake, spongecake, mohncake, cookies for a family gathering where everyone ate and drank—coffee, milk, cake—and later the talk still eddied among the women around the table or in the kitchen, while the men ended up in the living room watching the ball game. I had never known this kind of family. (*Blood, Bread, and Poetry* 115)

Although later Rich admitted that she had been objectifying her husband's family, which she considered "quintessentially and authentically Jewish," at the time these family gatherings provided her with something she felt she had been missing in her life (116). She believed that both her marriage and her participation in a Jewish culture were giving her the opportunity to "heal the split consciousness in which I had been raised, and, of course, to belong" (115).

four

Confines of Motherhood

A life I didn't choose
chose me

—Adrienne Rich, "The Roofwalker"

TWO YEARS AFTER SHE WAS MARRIED, Rich was pregnant with her first child. Before she was thirty years old, Rich gave birth to three sons over a period of five years. This was one of the most difficult periods in her life, both emotionally and artistically.

Marriage had seemed like a way for Rich to escape her father, connect to her Jewish roots, and fulfill society's expectations; however, shortly after she was married, Rich found married life for a woman in the 1950s to be confining and restrictive. Marriage soon seemed more like a trap than an escape. Despite the gains regarding the status of women made during the early part of the twentieth century, in the 1950s women were encouraged to fulfill traditional roles as mothers and wives, and to subordinate their lives to men. "[T]hese were the fifties, and in reaction to the earlier wave of feminism, middle-class women were making careers of domestic perfection, working to send their husbands through professional schools, then retiring to raise large families," Rich later observed in her essay "When We Dead Awaken" (*On Lies, Secrets, and Silence* 42). The country's postwar attitude advocated that women should limit their lives to the home and family, thus stifling any other kinds of opportunities. Rich found herself following in the footsteps of her own mother: giving up her art in order to take care of the children and to provide support for her husband's career.

Rich's first pregnancy was complicated by her fragile physical health and by the ongoing emotional strain with her parents. Two days before her son was born, Rich broke out in a rash, tentatively diagnosed as measles. Although there were no actual physical complications with the delivery itself, Rich felt physically and emotionally drained. She also felt isolated and lonely, and wished she had the support of her parents. Since her marriage, Rich had barely spoken to them, and she feared that a chasm had opened up between her and her father that would never be mended.

In the break in communication with her father, Rich and her mother had also stopped talking to each other. Now a mother herself, Rich realized how much she missed her own mother. However, Rich was too stubborn and afraid to ask for her: "Emerging from the fear, exhaustion, and alienation of my first childbirth, I could not admit even to myself that I wanted my mother, let alone tell her how much I wanted her" (*Of Woman Born* 222). In examining her complex relationship with her parents, Rich regretted that her problems with her father had also affected her ties to her mother: "For years, I felt my mother had chosen my father over me, had sacrificed me to his needs and theories" (222).

Shortly after Rich's first son, David Conrad, was born, her second book, *The Diamond Cutters and Other Poems* (1955), was published and received the Ridgely Torrence Memorial Award of the Poetry Society of America. The poems in *Diamond Cutters,* traditional in structure and subject, closely resemble the style of the poems in her first book. Consisting of many travel poems, *Diamond Cutters* records many of the famous sights and monuments Rich witnessed on her travels through Europe. Several of the poems also focus on more domestic and personal issues. For example, the poem "Living in Sin" explores a woman's growing dissatisfaction with her lover and her living situation:

> While she, jeered by minor demons,
> pulled back the sheets and made the bed and found
> a towel to dust the table top,
> and let the coffee-pot boil over on the stove.
> By evening she was back in love again

Most critics responded favorably to Rich's second collection. Poet Donald Hall stated in his review that although Rich's voice was still heavily influenced by Frost and Auden, "even if one should decide to dismiss these poems (which would be foolish), there would be many left to which one could attach no name but the author's own" (Cooper 212). Later in her life, Rich was self-critical of the poems in *Diamond Cutters,* calling them "facile and ungrounded imitations of other poets" and "exercises in style" (*Collected Early Poems* xx). However, in the eyes of the literary world, Rich was on her way to being an accomplished and well respected poet. She was quietly establishing herself as someone to be taken seriously, and others were noticing her success. The poet Sylvia Plath, for example, jealously measured herself against Rich's career. In one of her journals, she wrote: "Adrienne Cecile Rich: little, round & stumpy, all vibrant short black hair, great sparkling black eyes and a tulip-red umbrella: honest, frank, forthright & even opinionated" (Plath 368).

Unfortunately, after *Diamond Cutters,* the literary world would not hear from Rich for eight more years. Instead, Rich's life would be consumed by the responsibilities of motherhood. Rich had felt that marriage and motherhood were necessary for her personal fulfillment, for confirmation of her womanhood, but she discovered that she was emotionally and physically unprepared. The critic Paula Bennett points out that Rich was more like her father than she had thought, "ambitious, aggressive, demanding," and she had trouble adjusting to this way of life that seemed to immediately strip her of independence (Bennett 185).

In 1957, Rich's second son, Paul Conrad, was born, and her son Jacob followed two years later. In the beginning stages of motherhood, Rich struggled daily with waves of resentment toward her children, who were depriving her of her intellectual freedom. She felt angry that her children monopolized her time, and then felt ashamed for her anger, fearing that she was "monstrous" for experiencing anything short of delight toward her children. She realized that for many women, she was living the "American Dream," and thus felt guilty for feeling disappointment. However, she also could not deny the truth—that she often felt bored and depressed, and that she was constantly battling feelings of displacement and frustration. During this time, the mid-1950s, postnatal depression was still unheard of, and there were no women's groups or self-help books to lend support. As far as Rich knew, she was the only woman on earth who was feeling this way.

The isolation and loneliness was also aggravated by a developing confusion about her sexuality. Although Rich did not come out as a lesbian until after she had become active in the Women's Movement, she had already begun to question her sexuality in the early years of her marriage. She confided in Elly Bulkin in 1977 that she had actually written about her feelings for a woman in the "very guarded, carefully-wrought poem" "Stepping Backward," which appeared in her first book. "[T]hat poem is addressed to a woman whom I was close to in my late 'teens, and whom I really fled from—I fled from my feelings about her," said Rich. "It's very intellectualized, but it's really the first poem in which I was striving to come to terms with feelings for women" (Bulkin 64).

Not only did motherhood cause her to question who she was, but it also seriously threatened to end Rich's career as a poet. Although Rich had initially believed she could be both a poet and a mother, she found herself writing less and less: "I had stopped writing poetry, and read little except household magazines and books on child-care" (*Of Woman Born* 26). She went through a somber period in which she nearly stopped writing altogether. In a journal entry from 1956, she wrote, "Of late I've felt towards poetry—both reading it and writing it—nothing but boredom and indifference ... I have a strong sense of wanting to deny all responsibility for an interest in that person who writes—or who wrote" (26).

However, Rich's feelings of isolation and confinement slowly began to change once she became pregnant with her third child in July, 1958:

> About the time my third child was born, I felt I had either to consider myself a failed woman and a failed poet, or to try to find some synthesis by which to understand what was happening to me. What frightened me most was the sense of drift, of being pulled along on a current which called itself my destiny, but in which I seemed to be losing touch with whoever I had been, with the girl who had experienced her own will and energy almost ecstatically at times, walking around a city or riding a train at night or typing in a student room. (*On Lies, Secrets, and Silence* 42)

The Lavender Scare

In the height of McCarthyism and the second Red Scare, there was a growing verbalization against homosexuality. During this time instead of being asked the now famous question, "Are you now or have you ever been a member of the Communist Party?", citizens were being told, "Information has come to the attention of the Civil Service Commission that you are a homosexual. What comment do you care to make?". In February, 1950, 91 homosexuals, labeled "security risks," were forced to leave their jobs at the State Department at which point Deputy Undersecretary of State John Peurifoy appeared before Congress and announced that homosexuals in high government office posed a serious threat to national security.

Rich made the major decision to be sterilized after Jacob was born; this decision made his pregnancy easier to bear: "[B]y the time I knew I was pregnant with him, I was not sleepwalking anymore" (*Of Woman Born* 28). Despite others' disapproval, she felt confident that she had made the right decision, one in which she was exerting more control over her life and body. However, she was immediately reprimanded after the operation, when a young nurse scolded Rich. "When I awoke from the operation," Rich recalled, "a young nurse looked at my chart and remarked coldly: 'Had yourself spayed, did you?'" (30).

As her sons grew older, motherhood became less demanding, but while they were still young, Rich struggled daily with depression and feelings of inadequacy. She was exhausted by her recurrent flares of arthritis, the endless household chores, and the constant demands of her children. The journal she was writing in over the years reveals her near nervous breakdown. An entry dated November 1960 captures the push and pull of her emotions:

> My children cause me the most exquisite suffering of which I have any experience. It is the suffering of ambivalence: the murderous alternation between bitter resentment and raw-edged nerves, and blissful gratification and tenderness.... Their voices wear away at my nerves, their constant needs, above all their need for simplicity and patience, fill me with despair at my own failures, despair too at my fate, which is to serve a function for which I was not fitted. (*Of Woman Born* 21)

Exhausted from caring for her children and husband, and fearing she had lost all of her independence, Rich still found it difficult to acknowledge her anger. She did not blame her husband or children for her unhappiness, but instead held herself responsible for not being able to manage motherhood with her writing career: "[I]n those years I always felt the conflict as a failure of love in myself. I had thought I was choosing a full life: the life available to most men, in which sexuality, work, and parenthood could coexist. But I felt, at twenty-nine, guilty toward the people closest to me, and guilty toward my own being" (*On Lies, Secrets, and Silence* 44). It seemed impossible to be a poet—to explore her imagination and the pleasure of words—while having to fulfill the duties of motherhood. To be both a mother and a wife within the traditional structure of motherhood and marriage, Rich would later argue, "requires a holding back, a putting-aside of that imaginative activity" (43).

She felt distanced from her family, including her in-laws, whom she had been trying so hard to please by being a good wife, mother, and daughter–in-law. She felt torn about her identity, about gender roles and her cultural background: "I was encountering the institution of motherhood most directly in a Jewish cultural version; and I felt rebellious, moody, defensive, unable to sort out what was Jewish from what was simply motherhood or female destiny," she explained in "Split" (*Blood, Bread, and Poetry* 116). It seemed to Rich that the world was crashing around her, and the only solace she could find was when she was scribbling in notebooks or reading the work of others. She had what seemed like thousands of questions without answers, and she was "looking desperately for clues, because if there were no clues then I thought I might be insane" (*On Lies, Secrets, and Silence* 44).

It was around this time that Rich discovered the writing of the eighteenth century writer Mary Wollstonecraft, the French Existentialist Simone de Beauvoir, and the gay writer and Civil Rights activist James Baldwin, all of whom deeply influenced her thinking. "Each of them helped me to realize that what had seemed simply 'the way things are' could actually be a social construct, advantageous to some people and detrimental to others, and that these constructs could be criticized and changed," she explained in "Blood, Bread, and Poetry" (*Blood, Bread, and Poetry* 176).

Mary Wollstonecraft, a middle-class English woman, had written a plea for women and men to be treated equally in *Vindication of the Rights of Women*, and Simone de Beauvoir, two centuries later, showed how the male perception of "Woman as Other" had dominated European culture. De Beauvoir's *Second Sex* gave Rich the courage she needed to write about being a woman, and both of these writers were important in shaping Rich's thoughts about womanhood.

James Baldwin, the distinguished African-American author of such nonfiction books as *Notes of a Native Son* (1955) and *Nobody Knows My Name* (1961) and the novels *Giovanni's Room* (1956) and *Another Country* (1962), especially stirred Rich with his belief that "apparently 'given' situations like racism could be analyzed and described and that this could lead to action, to change" (*Blood, Bread, and Poetry* 118). Baldwin would be Rich's introduction to the Civil Rights movement, and his ideas also prompted her to question the status of women in American society.

[R]acism had been so utter and implicit a fact of my childhood and adolescence, had felt so central among the silences, negations, cruelties, fears, superstitions of my early life that somewhere among my feelings must have been the hope that if Black people could become free of the immense political and social burdens they were forced to bear, I, too, could become free of all the ghosts and shadows of my childhood, named and unnamed. (*Blood, Bread, and Poetry* 119)

All three of these writers, in their different ways, challenged Rich to think about the myths of race, gender, and sexuality, and it was during this time that Rich began to question the institution of motherhood, which would later form the thesis for her nonfiction book *Of Woman Born.*

Rich realized that she needed to find a non-traditional space that would allow her to be both mother and artist; otherwise, it would be impossible to be both: "But to be a female human being trying to fulfill traditional female functions in a traditional way *is* in direct conflict with the subversive function of the imagination," she asserted in *Of Woman Born* (174). In other words, a poet needs freedom of the mind and access to her own imagination to write poetry. However, when a woman is spending all of her time taking care of her children, the household, and her husband, it is nearly impossible to find a space in which to be able to fully explore her imagination. As a mother and a writer, Rich was never asking for the selfish "myth of the masculine artist and thinker," which was to become unavailable to others or to isolate oneself from family in order to pursue one's career. She did not want to abandon her family, but she did want time to write (*On Lies, Secrets, and Silence* 43).

During the 1950s, and even now, many women would argue, husbands had much more freedom than their wives. While Rich acknowledged that her husband, a caring, devoted father, was supportive of her, and that he encouraged her to pursue her poetry, she also believed that he did not fully grasp the depth of her emotional, mental, and physical exhaustion:

My husband was a sensitive, affectionate man who wanted children and who—unusual in the professional, academic world of the fifties—was willing to 'help.' But it was clearly understood that this 'help' was an act of generosity: that his work, his professional life, was the real work in the family; in fact, this was for years not even an issue between us. I understood that my struggles as a writer were a kind of luxury, a peculiarity of mine; my work brought in almost no money: it even cost money, when I hired a household helper to allow me a few hours a week to write. (*Of Woman Born* 27)

Furthermore, a woman's artistic or professional career was not taken as seriously as a man's. While men could always leave the house for work or social events, a woman was more restricted to the home and to the children. Rich realized she was falling into the same trap as her mother: she was giving up her art for her husband's career.

The confines of traditional marriage and motherhood began to slowly provoke Rich's politics, and although she would not formulate these ideas until later, Rich began to consider new possibilities for what motherhood could mean. One experience that exemplified these new possibilities arose one summer when she spent time at a friend's house in Vermont while her husband was working abroad for several weeks. Rich recalled how she and her sons experienced a new sense of freedom: "Without a male adult in the house, without any reason for schedules, naps, regular mealtimes, or early bedtimes so the two parents could talk, we fell into what I felt to be a delicious and sinful rhythm" (*Of Woman Born* 194).

Rich continued on with this way of life, slipping in and out of depression, and worrying that she'd given up writing poetry for good. However, sometime in the late 1950s, Rich found herself writing again in bits and pieces. These poems began moving in a different direction from her earlier poetry, and in 1956, to reveal these changes in her work, she began dating her poems, something she would continue to do throughout her career:

I did this because I was finished with the idea of a poem as a single, encapsulated event, a work of art complete in itself; I knew my life was changing, my work was changing, and I needed to indicate to readers my sense of being engaged in a long, continuous process. It seems to me now that was an oblique political statement—a rejection of the dominant critical idea that the poem's text should be read as separate from the poet's everyday life in the world. It was a declaration that placed poetry in a historical continuity, not above or outside history. (*Blood, Bread, and Poetry* 180)

By dating the poems, she was in a sense rejecting New Critical Theory, the most popular theory during this time; it places poetry outside of its cultural and historical context; The critic Liz Yorke asserts that for the first time Rich was writing about personal experiences, and this change in approach would ultimately affect the direction of her career: "Thus begins a lifelong allegiance to a poetry (and later, a theory) emerging out of lived experience—the actuality of personal, social and historical experience becomes both 'source and resource' for the work" (Yorke 10–11).

Uninterrupted time to write was never given to Rich; instead, like many women writers, she learned to write whenever she could find scraps of time. Then, over a period of two years, Rich wrote the famous ten-part poem, "Snapshots of a Daughter-in-Law" (1958–1960), a poem which symbolized a monumental change in her poetry. Most importantly, for the first time, Rich was able to write directly about experiencing herself as a woman. Furthermore, the looser, longer style itself liberated her. "It was an extraordinary relief to write that poem," she admitted (*On Lies, Secrets, and Silence* 45). Although she later criticized the voice for being too tentative—"It strikes me now as too literary, too dependent on

allusion; I hadn't found the courage yet to do without authori-
ties, or even to use the pronoun 'I'—the woman in the poem is
always 'she'"—Rich knew that this poem was what she had
needed to fuel her creativity and her career (*On Lies, Secrets,
and Silence* 45).

The return to writing poetry, however little she felt she was
completing, began to bring her more recognition and rewards.
She received various literary awards and honors, including the
National Institute of Arts and Letters Award for Poetry (1960)
and another Guggenheim Fellowship (1961–62), which gener-
ously allowed her to go with her family to the Netherlands. She
also received the prestigious Amy Lowell Travelling Fellowship
and a Bollingen Foundation grant to work on translations of
Dutch poetry while she was living in Amsterdam. (Since the
1950s Rich has been translating poetry from various languages,
including a large body of poems from Dutch.) When Rich and
her family returned to the United States, they bought a home
in Vermont and began spending their summers there, where
near-neighbors included the poets Galway Kinnell and Hayden
Carruth.

Then, after eight years of virtual silence, Rich's third book of
poems, *Snapshots of a Daughter in Law: Poems 1954–1962*
(1963), was published by W.W. Norton. It is still one of Rich's
most well known and beloved books, although at the time of
publication, most reviewers barely noticed it, and those that did
tended to give negative reviews or dismiss the writing as too
emotional. "I was seen as 'bitter' and 'personal'; and to be personal was to be disqualified, and that was very shaking because
I'd really gone out on a limb," Rich told Elly Bulkin. She
added, "I realized I'd gotten slapped over the wrists, and I didn't
attempt that kind of thing again for a long time" (Bulkin 50).
Rich had gone "out on a limb" with regard to the personal tone
and free-verse form of these new poems, which were quite

different from her earlier work. "It took me a long time not to hear those voices [of criticism] internally whenever I picked up my pen" (*Blood, Bread, and Poetry* 180).

Most contemporary critics regard *Snapshots*, which won the Bess Hokin Prize of *Poetry* magazine, as the point at which Rich's poetry changed direction. The poems in her first two books were traditional, Modernist-influenced; she had written them when she had "a much more absolutist approach to the universe" (*Adrienne Rich's Poetry and Prose* 165). But by the time she began writing *Snapshots*, she was questioning more about the world and about her life. She was no longer sure of who she was and felt confused about the decisions she'd made. The poems, as a result, are more open in style, resembling such modern poets as Sylvia Plath, Robert Lowell, and Denise Levertov, whom she had only recently been reading. The exposure to contemporary poets and her reading of philosophers and activists' work suggested to Rich "that life at this point is far too complicated and contradictory to be able to be tied up in a graceful sonnet" (Boland). The fact that she was no longer living under her father's influence perhaps also contributed to Rich's new voice and style. For so much of her life, Rich had been listening to her father, and his staunch, unwavering opinions on poetry had overshadowed her own poetic voice. Arnold Rich respected formalism and strict meters, but disdained free verse, and in the early part of her career, Rich had mostly written poetry that exemplified this viewpoint.

There were several critics who responded favorably to the book. In his review in the *Christian Science Monitor*, Philip Booth praised Rich for moving in unexplored territory: "The risk this book quietly takes, and impressively fulfills, is no less than to get life said" (Cooper 215). The critic Robert Boyers called it "surely her best book to date," adding that in these poems "Rich moves steadily to inhabit the world and to make contact with that self she had thought largely repressed and almost forgotten" (Cooper 150).

More informed by sexual politics than her first two books, *Snapshots* is also filled with personal reflection, as Rich examines her life as a mother and wife. Although she had feared she had lost herself when she became a mother, she was beginning to rediscover herself, emerging from the shadows and allowing herself to be seen. The title poem, which Rich called her "first overtly feminist poem" (Rothschild), focuses on the isolation of women in marriages, with a different speaker in each of the poem's ten sections. In Part One the first woman is most likely a reference to Rich's mother: "You, once a belle in Shreveport/with henna-colored hair, skin like a peachbud." The poem ends with a reference to the woman's daughter: "Nervy, glowering, your daughter/wipes the teaspoons, grows another way."

In the years to come, Rich would become more devoted to feminist politics and to dismantling patriarchal institutions. While her commitment to women's autonomy can be traced from even her earliest poems, it is in *Snapshots* that Rich first reveals her feminist leanings. In addition to the title poem, many of the poems in the book reference feminist mentors, such as Mary Wollstonecraft, Emily Dickinson, and Simone de Beauvoir. *Snapshots* was the first indicator that Rich was not the same poet who wooed the critics with her first book, *Change of World*. The poems in *Snapshots* symbolized a new direction in Rich's poetry, and also served as a wake-up call to the life she wanted to live. Soon following the publication of *Snapshots*, Rich started to become active in politics, fighting for social justice and equality. Although she did not fully realize it yet, *Snapshots* had marked the beginning of a major turn in her life.

five

Awakening to Politics

Even before I called myself a feminist or a lesbian, I felt driven—for my own sanity—to bring together in my poems the political world 'out there'—the world of children dynamited or napalmed, of the urban ghetto and militarist violence—and the supposedly private, lyrical world of sex and male/female relationships.

—Adrienne Rich, "Bread, Blood, and Poetry"

AFTER *SNAPSHOTS* WAS PUBLISHED, Rich felt that she had failed because of the critics who dismissed the book as "too bitter and personal," and, feeling reprimanded, she took a step back in her work, returning to the style of her earlier poems. Although *Necessities of Life: Poems 1962–1965* (1966) pleased critics and was nominated for the National Book Award, the poems, more traditional and "safer," in terms of style and subject, resembled her first book more than they did *Snapshots*. In the course of Rich's long career, however, the tone and style of *Necessities of Life* seems to have only been a pause during a turbulent period in her life and in the world. Rich's personal issues with motherhood, sexuality, and artistry were now being played against the larger background of the civil rights and antiwar movements. As these social and political movements gathered force during the 1960s, Rich became more actively involved, and her commitment to fighting for civil rights and her passionate antiwar sentiments began to directly affect the subject and themes of her poetry.

In 1966, the same year that Rich was named Phi Beta Kappa poet at Harvard, her family moved to New York so that Alfred could accept a teaching position at City College. The move represented a major change for the family: it meant leaving behind the liberal, academic milieu of Cambridge to live in a city that seemed to be literally on the verge of eruption. The mid-sixties was an explosive time to be living in New York. There were subway and cab strikes and a sanitation strike that left bags of uncollected trash piling up on the curbs and sidewalks. There were power and water shortages. Poor people were being evicted, and graffiti-covered tenements were demolished in order to build middle-class housing. All over the city there were protests and political demonstrations. Racism was prevalent, and white panic also took hold, with much of the white middle-class moving out.

Rich was disgusted with what she termed "white solipsism," in which privileged people, who were usually white and affluent, removed themselves from the daily workings of the city:

> [I]t was, and still is, possible to live, if you can afford it, on one of those small islands where the streets are kept clean and the pushers and nodders invisible, to travel by cab, deplore the state of the rest of the city, but remain essentially aloof from its cause and effects. It seems about as boring as most forms of solipsism, since to maintain itself it must remain thick-skinned and ignorant. (*On Lies, Secrets, and Silence* 54)

Stonewall

On June 28, 1969, police officers in New York City descended on the Stonewall Inn, a gay bar in Greenwich Village. Usually during these common raids, the cops threatened the gay clientele with public exposure and arrested a few people. However, this time, the two hundred patrons, consisting of mostly working class drag queens, gay men of color, and a few butch lesbians, congregated in front of the Stonewall and fought back.

As they staged the riot, their numbers quickly increased. Rioters threw bricks, bottles, and garbage from the Village streets, and before the night was over, four policemen were hurt. For the next two nights, police and protestors clashed in Sheridan Square, with fires starting all over the neighborhood, and cries to "support gay power" and "legalize gay bars" sounding across the night. These were the first gay riots in history. What came to be known as the Stonewall Rebellion was a rally for the Gay Liberation Movement, and became an emblem of gay and lesbian power.

Rich had no desire to remove herself from the city. She immediately felt energized by her new surroundings and liked being a part of the city's workings. The move to New York symbolized a significant change in Rich's life, as the urban environment incited her to become more politically involved and to also reexamine her views on the meaning of poetry.

The 1960s, a time of race riots, mass jailings, and police brutality, was also a time of intellectual, creative, and ideological ardor. There was a mood of exhilaration among the activists. "[T]here was a sense of hope that we could change this, that we could turn this around, we could stop the war, and we could not only stop the war there, but stop the war within our own boundaries," Rich later recalled (Boland). Both Rich and her husband were actively involved in the movements for social justice. At this point, Rich was not yet involved in feminism (the Women's Movement had not yet fully sprung into action), nor was she especially focused on exploring her Jewish roots. Most of Rich's political activities during the sixties were directed toward protesting the Vietnam War and supporting the Civil Rights Movement.

As the Civil Rights Movement gained power, Rich became more personally dedicated and politically astute. "When the Civil Rights Movement came along in the late fifties, early sixties, and I began to hear Black voices describing and analyzing what were the concrete issues for Black people, like segregation, like racism, it came to me as a great relief," she explained to David Montenegro. "It was like finding language for something that I'd needed a language for all along" (*Adrienne Rich's Poetry and Prose* 263). She had grown up in a place where racism was typical, and as a child she was aware of this, yet was unable to articulate her thoughts until much later. "I was born in the white section of a hospital that separated Black and white women in labor and Black and white babies in the nursery, just as it separated Black and white bodies in its morgue," Rich wrote. "I was defined as white before I was defined as female" (*Blood, Bread, and Poetry* 215). Although Baltimore did not have formal Jim Crow laws, segregation was an accepted way of life when Rich was growing up. Blacks and whites ate at separate restaurants, and did not intermingle in social situations.

Rich recalled the African-American nanny she had had until age four, who had cared for her as much as her own mother had, but who was restricted to a different class because of her race. "Two women, one white, one black, were the first persons I loved and who I knew loved me," she wrote in "It Is the Lesbian in Us" (*On Lies, Secrets, and Silence* 200). Now with the dynamism of the Civil Rights Movement, Rich had a more accurate lens in which to perceive her past, as well as the opportunity to join with others to fight for social justice. She saw how deeply racism was rooted in the workings of American society, but she believed that the Civil Rights Movement and the politics of the New Left, which consisted of intellectuals dedicated to sustaining a democratic and egalitarian socialist movement, would be able to shake up these foundations, to create lasting changes and provide equality for all citizens.

Although she was becoming more involved in left-wing politics, participating in protests and demonstrations, Rich was still very much a part of the elite literary world, where she continued to achieve more success. In 1967, her *Selected Poems* was published in Britain, and she also received an honorary doctorate degree from Wheaton College, the first of many honorary degrees for Rich. From 1967 to 1969, she was a lecturer at Swarthmore College. She was also an adjunct professor for the writing division at Columbia University, where she further immersed herself in the radical politics flooding the campus.

Then in 1968, Rich's experience with teaching changed

dramatically when she began teaching at the SEEK Program at City College. SEEK (Search for Education, Elevation and Knowledge) was a remedial English program created for open admissions students, who were mostly African American and Puerto Rican, entering the city college. Up until now, most of Rich's teaching experiences had taken place at Ivy League, liberal arts colleges, where the majority of the students were white and affluent. Teaching at SEEK opened Rich's eyes to a much different student population, and through this job, she was exposed to more social and political movements. She notes in "Teaching Language in Open Admissions" that she started the job the same year Martin Luther King was assassinated:

> I applied for the job at City in 1968 because Robert Cumming had described the SEEK program to me after Martin Luther King was shot, and my motivation was complex. It had to do with white liberal guilt, of course; and a political decision to use my energies in work with "disadvantaged" (black and Puerto Rican) students. But it also had to do with a need to involve myself with the real life of the city, which had arrested me from the first weeks I began living here. (*On Lies, Secrets, and Silence* 53)

Although teaching in SEEK was more difficult than she had initially imagined, Rich was devoted to her students' learning. "The early experience in SEEK was, as I look back on it, both unnerving and seductive," she admitted (*On Lies, Secrets, and Silence* 55). The experience profoundly changed her and deepened her commitment to the Civil Rights Movement. She felt that she learned from her students as much as they learned from her. "[O]ur white liberal assumptions were shaken," she said of herself and her white colleagues, "our vision of both the city and the university changed, our relationship to language itself made both deeper and more painful" (57). The SEEK program revealed to Rich how the personal and lived experiences and political and social discourses were connected to each other.

One of Rich's first romantic notions of teaching was formed when she was a teenager and read the play "The Corn is Green" by Emlyn Williams. In it a devoted teacher "discovers" a writer among her students and encourages him to seek education. As Rich spent more time with her SEEK students, her early naïve views on teaching grew into a sophisticated, intelligent perspective that was grounded in both realism and hope: "What interests me in teaching is less the emergence of the occasional genius than the overall finding of language by those who did not have it and by those who have been used and abused to the extent that they lacked it" (*On Lies, Secrets, and Silence* 67–68). The complexity of language shows up as a theme in much of Rich's work. She examines the ways in which language offers freedom as well as oppression. With SEEK, she found herself encountering students who had been marginalized and neglected by the system, and she wanted to give them language as a tool, to help them discover their voices.

An ambitious and devoted teacher, Rich turned on her students to writing and reading by various methods, including poetry, free association, music, politics, drama, and fiction. She chose a wide range of books by both traditional and newer experimental authors including George Orwell, Richard Wright, LeRoi Jones (now Amiri Baraka), D.H. Lawrence, James Baldwin, and Plato. At this point, there were not many books by black women writers that were available at bookstores, although the shelves were certainly crowded with the writings of black men. Rich brought the work of Malcolm X, Langston Hughes, W.E.B DuBois, and Eldridge Cleaver into the classroom. Later she would come to know and admire the

work of African-American women authors, including June
Jordan and Toni Cade Bambara, both of whom were also SEEK
teachers, as well as Gwendolyn Brooks and Audre Lorde. All of
these women contributed to her understanding of race and
racism, as well as feminism.

The year 1968 was an intensely political time, with the
country shaken by the assassinations of Martin Luther King
and Robert Kennedy. It was also a year of profound personal
loss for Rich when her father, who had been struggling with a
long deteriorating illness, died on April 17, 1968. After she
had given birth to her children, Rich reconnected with her
parents and re-established her relationship with them. During
his last few years, it had been difficult for her to watch her
father's decline. He had almost entirely lost his sight, and by
the end of his life, he was also losing his capacity to think.
According to Rich, as her father became more ill, he withdrew
further into isolation, refusing to interact with anyone outside
the family: "In his home, he created a private defense so elab-
orate that even as he was dying, my mother felt unable to talk
freely with his colleagues or others who might have helped
her" (*Blood, Bread, and Poetry* 114). In the touching poem
"After Dark," addressed to her dying father, Rich documents
the experience of witnessing him slowly lose his life: "I seem
to hold you, cupped/in my hands, and disappearing." The
poem expresses the depth of Rich's love for her father, and also
exposes how in some way his death may have liberated her:
"You are falling asleep and I sit looking at you/old tree of
life/old man whose death I wanted/I can't stir you up now."
Her father's death left her stricken with grief and feeling profoundly displaced. Yet, as she would explore years later in the
poem "Sources," her father was still very much a part of her
life, and even after his death, she was still engaged in a dialogue with him: "[H]e and I always had a/kind of rhetoric

going with each other, a battle between us, it didn't/matter if one of us was alive or dead."

One year after her father's death, Rich's fifth book of poetry, *Leaflets: Poems 1965–1968* (1969), was published. One of her most overtly political books, *Leaflets* documents the political upheavals of the 1960s, including the Vietnam War and civil rights revolutions in the United States. In critic Wendy Martin's opinion, the book "reflects [Rich's] growing awareness of the profound connection between private and public life" and the poems, many of them angry and revolutionary in tone, reveal "that poetry and politics are intertwined—that poetry has the power to transform lives" (Martin 185). The poems, many composed in a fragmentary two-space line, also reveal how Rich was becoming more wedded to ideas of feminism, and unveil Rich's own "awakening" after motherhood, how she was rethinking her concepts of gender and sexuality. The more open, experimental structure of the poems also matched the complicated subjects she was trying to talk about. She knew at this point she could never return to the neat forms that appeared in her first book: "Experience itself had become too much for that" (*Adrienne Rich's Poetry and Prose* 269).

The poem "Orion" reveals Rich's continuing struggle against the confines of her marriage, her rediscovery of herself during motherhood, and her longing to possess as much freedom as men. The speaker yearns to be outside with the cold, burning star, "my fierce half-brother," and away from indoors where "A man reaches behind my eyes/And finds them empty" and "children are dying my death/and eating crumbs of my life." Rich later analyzed this poem in her essay "When We Dead Awaken," calling it "a poem of reconnection with a part of myself I had felt I was losing—the active principle, the energetic imagination, the "half-brother" whom I projected, as I had for many years, into the constellation Orion" (*On Lies, Secrets, and Silence* 45).

Like the other poets of her generation, including Denise Levertov, Robert Bly, and W.S. Merwin, Rich wrote poems that reflected the social upheaval of the late sixties and early seventies, and yet her work also differed from the other political poets because she was also writing about women. Even while adamantly protesting Vietnam and racism, she was examining gender inequality and oppression: "At the same time, I was thinking a lot about something that wasn't being talked about at the time very much. I was thinking about where sexuality belonged in all this. What is the connection between Vietnam and the lover's bed?" (*Adrienne Rich's Poetry and Prose* 263). The poem "Nightbreak," for example, links personal oppression with the terror of war:

> In the bed the pieces fly together
> and the rifts fill   or else
> my body is a list   of wounds
> symmetrically placed
> a village
> blown open   by planes
> that did not   finish the job.

Rich was raised in a conservative upper-class family, and all her life, her parents and relatives taught her that women must be submissive and polite. Rich's new poems questioned these attitudes. Although during these years Rich spent most of her energy protesting the war and fighting for civil rights, the meaning of marriage and the desire for independence were a growing part of her consciousness, and soon these concerns would dominate both her political involvement and her personal life.

SIX

A Community of Women

The women's movement appeared at a very crucial moment in my life ... I began to feel heard in that movement. But it was because my voice was resonating with other voices.

—Adrienne Rich, in an interview with Paulo da Costa

ADRIENNE RICH WAS A WIFE and mother during one of the most conservative decades in America, and at the time these roles seemed like the only feasible path for a woman to take. Soon after marriage, she realized how stifling the arrangement was, but she felt there was nothing she could do to change the situation. Along with marriage came motherhood, which had also been tremendously difficult. Nearly ending her career as a poet, motherhood had aroused complicated feelings of depression, guilt, love, and anger. Like most women during the fifties, Rich felt isolated in her experience, as if she were the only woman in America struggling with these feelings. "Life was extremely private; women were isolated from each other by marriage," she later wrote. "I have a sense that women didn't talk to each other much in the fifties—not about their secret emptiness, their frustrations" (*On Lies, Secrets, and Silence* 42). She only knew she wanted something more, something that marriage or motherhood could not give her.

Then, in the early sixties, during the heated time of the Civil Rights Movement and the protests against Vietnam, the temper of America greatly changed and women began to speak out about their dissatisfaction with their own lives. Their voices sent quiet ripples across the country, but it was not until 1963, when Betty Friedan, a housewife and former labor union journalist, published the landmark book *The Feminine Mystique,* that women all over America began to be more vocal about their growing discontent.

In *The Feminine Mystique* Friedan argued that women in America were only defined in relation to men, and that the "mystique" was a fictitious, powerful belief system of femininity. She interviewed hundreds of educated suburban housewives, who spoke about their feelings of boredom, oppression, and depression, and who questioned the meaning of their existence. All of these women thought that what they were feeling was unique to them, and often blamed themselves for their unhappiness. This was a time when abortions were illegal and marital rape was legal. Politicians didn't address women's issues, and many universities had male-only admissions policies. Newspaper help-wanted columns were separated

Feminists Battle for Legal Rights

The Women's Liberation Movement transformed individual lives as well as the country's political landscape. During the sixties and seventies, women fought to change many discriminatory practices and laws in the United States, participating in numerous protests, strikes, sit-ins, and other demonstrations.

Their dedication and determination paid off in many areas. Newspapers stopped sex-segregated advertising, and major companies agreed to end discrimination in salaries. Most states made marital rape illegal, and in 1973, the monumental decision of Roe v. Wade granted women the right to legally chose abortion.

Despite these successes, one of the major disappointments was the failure of the ERA. The Equal Rights Amendment, which had been drafted in 1923, was finally passed in Congress after fifty years. The amendment, which states, "Equality of rights under the law shall not be denied or abridged by the United States or by any State on account of sex," was sent on to the states for ratification. To many women's rights activists, its ratification by the required thirty-eight states seemed like a given.

However, a severe backlash, led by ERA-opponent Phyllis Schlafly, swept the country, and despite polls consistently showing a large majority of the population supporting the ERA, it was considered by many politicians to be too controversial. In 1982, the Equal Rights Amendment died when it fell three states short of the thirty-eight needed to write the amendment into the U.S.Constitution.

by sex (with women offered only the dead-end jobs), and women were usually not granted bank loans or credit cards without their husband's endorsement. Marriage was one of the only ways for many women to obtain economic support.

The Feminine Mystique became an immediate bestseller and soon inspired thousands of women to look for fulfillment beyond the role of homemaker. That same year, Title VII of the 1964 Civil Rights Act was passed, prohibiting employment discrimination on the basis of sex as well as race, religion, and national origin. The tide began to turn for women, who were no longer sitting quietly in their kitchens. They began to find each other, to speak to the public and politicians about the way women were discriminated against, silenced, and exploited.

For many women, the exposure to activism was an entirely new experience. However, the majority of feminist leaders had previously been active in the New Left, civil rights, antiwar, and other counterculture movements, from which they were expecting to receive mutual support. On the issue of promoting social justice for women, the New Left abandoned them, blatantly belittling their cause. Feminists soon became disenchanted with what they saw as a male-dominated, patriarchal group, and they broke apart to form their own movement, one which would radicalize women all over America.

In 1966, the National Organization for Women (NOW), led by Friedan, officially started. This organization had a dues-paying membership that worked within the structures of society to change laws and attitudes; its members quickly became effective lobbyists and organizers. The names that began to appear in the media as major leaders of the feminist movement were Betty Friedan, Kate Millet, Germaine Greer, and *Ms.* magazine founder (1972) Gloria Steinem. However, there was another growing wing of the Women's Movement that did not belong to an established organization. These radical-feminists offered a more extreme critique of patriarchal culture and visions of alternative lifestyles; they often worked outside established institutions. The radical-feminists were usually younger women, who often used shock tactics and revolutionary ideas to fight patriarchy and were unconcerned about being accepted by mainstream culture. Although the radical-feminists were arguably the stronger force in the movement, both reformers and radicals worked in different ways to change the laws and attitudes of American society.

The common effort of all types of women to invigorate and strengthen the Women's Liberation movement helped revolutionize America during the late sixties and early seventies. These were important years for women; small groups in hundreds of communities across the United States worked on grassroots projects. They established women's bookstores, opened cafes, and started newspapers and presses. They set up childcare centers, battered women's shelters, rape crises hotlines, and clinics offering birth control and abortion services. They protested and picketed all over the country, and were instrumental in changing laws, including the legalization of abortion and the guarantee of equal opportunity in the workforce.

For Adrienne Rich, who had been so active in the Civil Rights Movement and other causes of the New Left, the understanding that women were now fighting for equality motivated her to take action. In the late sixties and early seventies, Rich became more involved in and closely identified with the burgeoning Women's Movement and feminist politics. "I had been looking for the Women's Liberation Movement since the 1950s," she wrote in the foreword to *Blood, Bread, and Poetry*. "I came into it in 1970" (vii). In August of that year, NOW and radical-feminists put aside their differences to take part in the National Women's Strike for Equality. Rich recalled that thousands of women marched in New York City and although she was not a part of the march (she was with her family in Vermont), she suddenly knew that this was the sort of empowerment among women for which she had been yearning.

As the Women's Movement grew stronger, weaving itself into the tapestry of American society, feminism began to move to the forefront of both Rich's poetry and her political commitment. Although this period marks a significant change in Rich's life, it was not a sudden transition. That is to say, feminist ideas had already appeared in many of the poems in *Leaflets* as well as in earlier poems, such as the memorable "Snapshots of a Daughter-in-Law." Her commitment to the Women's Liberation Movement seemed like a natural progression of her personal and political concerns; what was different was that she was no longer alone.

Now, for the first time in her life, Rich found herself part of a supportive community of other women, in which politics and personal issues overlapped. Earlier in her life, when she was trying to write while raising her three sons, she had little social support. Now she began attending meetings for women, reading groups, and political discussions, and she felt less alone in her life. "[T]he women's movement connected for me with the conflicts and concerns I'd been feeling when I wrote *Snapshots of a Daughter-in-Law*, as well as with the intense rapid politicization of the 1960s New Left. It opened up possibilities, freed me from taboos and silences, as nothing had ever done; without a feminist movement I don't see how I could have gone on growing as a writer," she explained to Elly Bulkin (Bulkin 51).

The move to New York had first incited Rich to become involved in politics, radicalizing her beliefs and awareness of injustices. Initially, her husband had also been a part of this lifestyle. Supportive of Rich's growing activism, Alfred had joined his wife in hosting radical anti-Vietnam and Black Panther fundraising parties at their New York apartment. But eventually, Alfred began to feel distanced from Rich's new commitments. As Rich became more involved in the Women's Liberation Movement, Alfred began to feel isolated from her. The poet Hayden Carruth, a close friend of the Riches, said that as Rich became politically active, tension increased in the marriage: "She was becoming a very pronounced, very militant feminist. I don't know what went on between them, except that Alf came to me and complained bitterly that Adrienne had lost her mind" (O'Mahoney).

From Rich's perspective, the marriage was stifling and suffocating, and she felt more and more trapped with each passing day. As she realized how radically split she felt from herself, as a mother and wife, she began to move further away from the tradition of marriage, entering a time of personal transformation. Most likely at this point her questions about her sexuality were growing more intense, and she was discovering, through the meetings and interactions with women, that there were other possibilities and choices. Most importantly, Rich sought independence and autonomy, and she knew that her marriage would never allow her this freedom. She resented how much time she had given up to support her husband, and how this level of support had not been returned to her. Tensions increased between Rich and her husband. Both of them were indulging in affairs, and growing more frustrated and dissatisfied with each other. Finally, the marriage reached a breaking point. In the summer of 1970, Rich made a monumental decision: after seventeen years of marriage, she left her family and moved into a small apartment nearby.

A few months after Rich's departure, Alfred, who was seeing

a therapist and struggling with depression over the break-up of the marriage and career difficulties, would do something drastic and irrevocable. One day in October, after months of upheaval, Alfred left the city for what he assured his children would be a brief trip. When he didn't return, Rich grew worried and she called Hayden Carruth, who still lived close to the Rich family summer house in Vermont. Carruth vividly recalled the morning he received Rich's phone call:

> She said he had taken off, possibly to Vermont. I drove to their place and couldn't find him, so I left a note on the door. The next day the cops called and asked me to come and help identify his body. Immediately after that I called and told her. She wasn't unprepared. Alf was going to a psychiatrist at the time and one reason he came up to Vermont was that he couldn't get hold of his psychiatrist in New York. It was very complicated. I think that temperamental differences had something to do with it. I think Alf was a disappointed person, who, as Adrienne became more celebrated, became more depressed. (O'Mahoney)

On that brisk October morning, Alfred Conrad left his family, rented a car, went to a meadow near their home in Vermont, and shot himself.

For years Rich said very little to the public about her feelings about her husband's suicide, but more recently, she has spoken about the impact this tragedy had on her and her sons' lives: "It was shattering for me and my children," she said (O'Mahoney). "It was a tremendous waste. He was a man of enormous talents and love of life." It would take Rich fifteen years before she could write about her husband's suicide, which she did in the poignant autobiographical poem "Sources." In the long poem Rich examines the way her father's and husband's lives impacted her, and in one of the prose sections, she addresses her husband with deep love and sorrow:

> ..... no person
> trying to take responsibility for her or his identity, should have to be so alone. There must be those among whom we can sit down and weep, and still be counted as warriors. (I make up this strange, angry packet for you, threaded with love.) I think you thought there was no such place for you, and perhaps there was none then, and perhaps there is none now; but we will have to make it, we who want an end to suffering ...

Rich faced this devastating loss with strength and determination. Over the years, Rich has shown herself to be a fierce survivor. "She has huge energy," the poet Jean Valentine said. "She's had to go through an awful lot of stuff and she's kept her head up" (O'Mahoney).

During this time of intense grief, Rich relied upon the support of her women friends and cut off most of her male acquaintances. Carruth found himself cast out of Rich's world for several years: "We are as close friends as you are likely to find. But Adrienne is very quick-tempered, very defensive and egomaniacal in many ways, and hard to get along with" (O'Mahoney). A decade later, Rich explained to Carruth that she was bothered by the male friends of her husband's, who were coming around after her husband's death, and said she felt "repressed and disgusted" (O'Mahoney). She spent most of her time with her women friends and her three sons, helping her children to sort through their feelings of grief, anger, and loss. She grew closer to her sons, and the four of them, in the wake of Alfred's suicide, took care of each other: "In time my sons grew older, I began changing my own life, we began to talk to each other as equals. Together we lived through my leaving the marriage, and through their father's suicide. We became survivors, four distinct people with strong bonds connecting us" (*Of Woman Born* 32).

As Rich tried to heal herself and her family after Arnold's suicide, she also struggled with inchoate feelings of sadness, guilt, and anger. Both the women's community and poetry offered her support and a place to articulate her endless questions about her life and the world. "I have known a good many kinds of loneliness in my life; but far more of it before I began to reach out to a community of women with whom I could relate through work as well as emotionally, where we can exchange resources on the same lifeline, as it were," she once told an interviewer (Boyd 14). The critic Paula Bennett suggests that Alfred's death marked the closing of a chapter in Rich's life: "When she picked up writing again, her voice and style had once more changed profoundly but this time in ways that would allow her, finally, to make her poetry her own" (Bennett 209).

The impact of this personal, political, sexual revolution was apparent in Rich's next book, *The Will to Change: Poems 1968–1970* (1971), which won the Shelley Memorial Award of the Poetry Society of America. The poems included in this volume chronicle the personal and the political, and are sometimes filled with rage toward what Rich increasingly saw as a sexist, patriarchal society. This rage was not unique to Rich—a newly discovered anger among women helped drive the Women's Movement to action. As the feminist historian Ruth Rosen explained, "American women had believed they were among the most emancipated women in the world.... Discovering their subordinate status suddenly threw everything in doubt" (Rosen 198). The voice and subject matter of Rich's poems had changed significantly from her first book. It was obvious that Rich was no longer imitating her elders; she had outgrown the Modernist poets, and her poems, bold and confident, continued to take on new territories and to express these ideas in a voice that was wholly unique to Rich.

Rich's feminist allegiances are obvious in poems such as "Planetarium," which celebrates the nineteenth-century astronomer Caroline Herschel, whose life and work were overshadowed by her brother William: "A woman in the shape of a monster/a monster in the shape of a woman/the skies are full of them." Many of the poems in this volume also hold a close lens to Rich's own experiences and reveal the complications in her life during this time. "Shooting Script," a poem in fourteen-parts, including sections of prose, white space, and broken images, describes a character who has encountered struggles and missteps, but who continues to survive: "To reread the instructions on your palm; to find there/how the life line, broke, keeps its direction." According to the critic Wendy Martin, the fragmented lines and images "reflect the discontinuity of Rich's life during this period.... The familiar pattern of the poet's life has been disrupted: the words crack, split, broken fracture, express this fragmentation. But from the shards of her old life comes the beginning of a new pattern" (Martin 187). The poem's imagistic and broken style also reflects Rich's growing interest in film and photography. During the 1960s, she went to more films than she had before, which influenced her work and inspired the poem "Images for Godard."

The poems in *The Will to Change*, in a myriad of images and themes, contemplate the power and complexity of both relationships and language. The critic David Kalstone claims that this book and others that follow "seem driven by the craving for new ways of talking, so that the asserted, palpable self might be accepted as the basis of relation between lovers, husband and wife, friends" (Kalstone 154). In the powerful poem "The

Burning of Paper Instead of Children," Rich examines the ambiguity of language, how it is used to express both love and oppression: "this is the oppressor's language/yet I need it to talk to you."

Although Rich had not yet come out as a lesbian, she was questioning her sexuality and examining how her personal life connected to her political beliefs. She had already sensed that nothing about her involvement in the Women's Movement was going to be easy, that it would take a great courage on her part. By now, Rich had heard lesbians speaking out within the Women's Movement, and she was aware of the early lesbian manifestoes. She explained how this new visibility and activism of lesbians impacted her immediately: "I had known very early on that the women's movement was not going to be a simple walk across an open field; that it would pull on every fiber of my existence; that it would mean going back and searching the shadows of my consciousness" (*Blood, Bread, and Poetry* 121).

As Rich grew more connected to the ideas of the radical-feminists, she felt that she was discovering her true self. Being a poet, a mother, and a woman no longer seemed irreconcilable. "To write directly and overtly as a woman, out of a woman's body and experience, to take women's existence seriously as theme and source for art, was something I had been hungering to do, needing to do, all my writing life," Rich explained. "But it released tremendous energy in me, as in many other woman, to have that way of writing affirmed and validated in a growing political community. I felt for the first time the closing gap between poet and woman" (*Blood, Bread, and Poetry* 182).

Rich became an outspoken member of the Women's Liberation Movement, involving herself in conferences, protests, and consciousness-raising meetings, in which small groups of women met to explore the political aspects of personal life. In sharing their stories with each other, they discovered a community, and consciousness-raising became a principal aspect of the Women's Liberation Movement. Much of Rich's work during this period reflected this major philosophy of the Women's Movement—that the political could be discovered within the personal, and that community was more powerful than the individual—and she contributed to the movement through her poems, essays, and various speaking engagements.

In 1971, Rich participated in a panel discussion sponsored by the Commission on the Status of Women in the Profession, along with several other women writers, including the feminist Tillie Olsen, author of *Tell Me A Riddle*. The panel presented views on "The Woman Writer in the Twentieth Century." When it was her turn to present, Rich read her now famous essay, "When We Dead Awaken: Writing as Re-Vision." The essay, one of Rich's most quoted, stresses that "re-vision—the act of looking back, of seeing with fresh eyes, of entering an old text from a new critical direction" could offer women historical visibility, political power, and survival. In order to persevere, women had to actively reject the confines of a patriarchal society (*On Lies, Secrets, and Silence* 35). The essay served as a call to action: "And this drive to self-knowledge, for women, is more than a search for identity: it is part of our refusal of the self-destructiveness of male-dominated society" (35).

Although Rich's prose and speeches were the most evident examples of her radical politics, her poetry during this time also clearly reflected her growing connection to feminist politics, her desire for women's equal rights, and her commitment to examining and dismantling the patriarchal nature of American society. In her poem "Trying to Talk with a Man," written the same year as the essay "Re-Vision," Rich explores the breakdown between men and women and portrays the dominance and power of a man over a woman. Beginning with the startling line, "Out in this desert we are testing bombs," the poem juxtaposes the violence of weaponry with a male-female relationship:

> Your dry heat feels like power
> your eyes are stars of a different magnitude
> they reflect lights that spell out: EXIT
> when you get up and pace the floor

Another poem written during the same time period is the ten-part poem "The Phenomenology of Anger," in which Rich directs her anger toward the violence of the Vietnam War and male power: "—at once the most destructive/and the most elusive being/gunning down the babies at My Lai." Rich describes "meeting the enemy" in a fury of violent images:

> white acetylene
> ripples from my body
> effortlessly released
> perfectly trained
> on the true enemy
>
> raking his body down to the thread
> of existence
> burning away his lie
> leaving him in a new
> world; a changed
> man

The poem offers no forgiveness, allows no mercy. Instead, the images seize on the way Rich felt women's collective anger could be used to change society. "I think anger can be a kind of genius if it's acted on," Rich once said (Rich, *Adrienne Rich's Poetry* 111).

Both of these poems were collected in Rich's next book of published poems, *Diving into the Wreck* (1973), which astounded many critics and readers for its depth and beauty. The poems proclaim the importance of a community of women, and also explore the layers of meanings of personal identity. Some of the poems, especially in Part III, are angry in tone, rebelling against patriarchal power structures; yet at the same time, there is an intimacy found in this work, as Rich explores her own identity and what it means to be a woman in this world. "It is here that Rich makes her strongest political identification with feminism, in her attempts to define experiences unique to women or to define the damages done by false definitions of sexual identity," asserts the critic David Kalstone. "Into her images she has been able to concentrate much of what has always been in her poetry: what it is like to feel oppressed, betrayed and unfulfilled" (Kalstone 162).

One of the strongest reviews published in a mainstream publication came from the renowned Canadian poet and novelist Margaret Atwood in the *New York Times Book Review*. Calling the poems "extraordinary," Atwood pointed out how the book blends politics with the personal without being didactic or preachy:

If Adrienne Rich were not a good poet, it would be easy to classify her as just another vocal Women's Libber, substituting polemic for poetry, simplistic messages for complex meanings. But she is a good poet, and her book is not a manifesto, though it subsumes manifestoes; nor is it a proclamation, though it makes proclamations. It is instead a book of explorations, of travels. (*Adrienne Rich's Poetry and Prose* 280)

The novelist Erica Jong also praised Rich for being political without losing her artfulness: "Rich is now one of the very few poets who can deal with political issues in her poems without letting them degenerate into socialist realism, because her notion of politics is not superficial; it is essentially psychological and organic" (Cooper 171). With its intelligence and depth Rich's work stood apart from the more moralizing poetry to come out of the Women's Movement. Although a few negative reviews appeared, most critics praised the poems, and many still view this book, especially the title poem, as a turning point in Rich's career. The book was important for the canon of American poetry and also marked a transformation for Rich.

"Diving into the Wreck" is one of Rich's strongest poems, what the critic Ruth Whitman calls "one of the great poems of our time" (Cooper 243). The poem describes the changes a woman has undergone in her personal life, revealing the woman's inner strength and her desire to know her own life.

I am having to do this
not like Cousteau with his
assiduous team
aboard the sun-flooded schooner
but here alone.
....
I came to explore the wreck.
The words are purposes.
The words are maps.
I came to see the damage that was done
and the treasures that prevail.
....
This is the place
And I am here, the mermaid whose dark hair
streams black, the merman in his armored body
We circle silently

about the wreck
we dive into the hold
I am she: I am he.

The narrator of the poem—a survivor—looks closely and
deeply at the disaster, learning from it instead of running away;
through this courage, is able to rediscover herself. The sugges-
tion of androgyny also appears as a way to help one find
wholeness. In order not to be "split," one must have both male
and female characteristics, a concept that Rich will later
denounce. This was a poem that spoke to many people. In an
essay examining Rich's impressive career, Helen Vendler focuses
on this particular poem, asserting, "The forcefulness of *Diving
into the Wreck* comes from the wish not to huddle wounded,
but to explore the caverns, the scars, the depths of the
wreckage" (*Adrienne Rich's Poetry and Prose* 310). "Diving"
reveals Rich's survivor skills, her courage in examining and
facing the transformations in her life with a critical, compas-
sionate gaze.

Diving into the Wreck was awarded the National Book Award
in 1974. However, Rich rejected the award as an individual and
would only accept it if the award was also given to the other
women nominees, Audre Lorde and Alice Walker, two African-
American writers. Rich's demand startled many in the literary
society, but for her it seemed only right that she emphasize and
recognize the importance of a community of women over the
accomplishments of an individual artist. Thus, together, the
three women authors wrote an acceptance statement on behalf
of all women:

We ... together accept this award in the name of all women
whose voices have gone and still go unheard in a patriarchal
world, and in the name of those who, like us, have been

tolerated as token women in this culture, often at great cost and in great pain ... We dedicate this occasion to the struggle for self-determination of all women, of every color, identification or derived class. (*Adrienne Rich's Poetry*, 204)

By refusing to accept such a major award for herself, Rich revealed that her allegiances to the feminist movement were much stronger and deeper than her connection to the literary world, which she viewed as male-dominated and elitist. The act also exemplifies how strongly Rich believed in the necessity and power of a diverse community of women. "I think women have a mission to survive ... and to be whole people," she told Wendy Martin in a personal interview. "I believe that this can save the world, but I don't think that women have a mission to clean up after men's messes. I think we have to save the world by doing it for ourselves—for all women—I don't mean some narrow, restricted notion of who women are, only white women or only middle-class women and only Western women" (Martin 232).

To Rich, a supportive, vibrant community was more powerful than a single individual could ever hope to be, and this is a belief that has deepened for her over the years, becoming an indispensable part of her philosophy and poetic sensibility.

chapter
seven

Coming Out

Heterosexuality as an institution has also drowned in silence the erotic feelings between women. I myself lived half a lifetime in the lie of that denial. That silence makes us all, to some degree, into liars.

—Adrienne Rich, "Women and Honor: Some Notes on Lying"

ALONG WITH HER POLITICAL ACTIVISM, teaching continued to be an important part of Rich's writing career. From 1972–73, she was the Fanny Hurst Visiting Professor of Creative Literature at Brandeis University, and in 1975, she was a Lucy Martin Donnelley Fellow at Bryn Mawr College. At this point, Rich was also becoming a more familiar name among poetry readers and literary critics. Most viewed her as an accomplished poet with a blossoming career, despite the feminist ideas that were appearing in her work. Following the critical success of *Diving,* a Norton anthology of her poems appeared in 1975. That same year, Rich's *Poems Selected and New 1950–1974* was also published, and in a review in *Harvard Magazine,* Ruth Whitman praised the progression of Rich's poetry: "If [Rich] began in 1951 with a control that seemed to me to be cold, she has exploded into passion and compassion, beginning in 1966 when she moved to New York from Cambridge ... if her poetry is now open and even occasionally violent, it carries with it the strength of those years of craft" (Cooper 242).

One of the new poems that appeared in the collection was "From an Old House in America" in which Rich chides her critics, "If they call me man-hater, you/would have known it for a lie." As Rich was stepping up as a leader of the Women's Movement, she felt she could no longer separate politics from her personal life: women's liberation was a part of her very being. "I feel as if my life and work are completely intertwined," she said (Boyd 15). It was as if the movement had opened a window for her, giving her the necessary air to breathe, and she realized this sense of belonging and purpose was what she had been waiting for so much of her life. The final line of the poem, "Most of the time, in my sex, I was also alone," expresses the isolation Rich had felt for most of her life up until now.

As Rich continued to devote her energy to the Women's Lib-eration Movement and feminist politics, on a personal level, she began also to examine her sexuality. To many of her friends, the revelation that Rich was a lesbian came as a shock, but others did not seem surprised, finding coded references in early poems. For example, Rich wrote about her love for a woman in "To Judith, Taking Leave" in 1962, although the poem did not appear until 1975, when it was collected in *Poems: Selected and New*. "It was a period in my life when I was very much in love with a woman and not calling it by that name," Rich said later (Bulkin 60). She explained that when she wrote the poem, she did not consider it a "lesbian" poem.

> This is what I have to keep reminding myself—that at that time I did not recognize, I did not name the intensity of those feelings as I would name them today, we did not name them. But my dismissing of it was akin to my dis-missing of the relationship, although in some ways I did not dismiss it—it was very much with me for a very long time. In 1962 there was precious little around to support the notion of the centrality of a relationship between two women. (Bulkin 65)

Rich herself was not surprised by her decision to come out of the closet, as she had been privately questioning her sexuality for years. It seemed that she was finally fulfilling her desires that had lain dormant for years. By Rich's account, she decided to act on her sexual feelings for women only after she read Judy Grahn's poem "A Woman Is Talking to Death." It was January, 1974, and she was home in bed, sick with the flu, when she came across the poem in *Amazon Quarterly*, a lesbian literary journal. The long, complicated poem suggests that if women give their love and loyalty to men instead of each other, then they are giving themselves to death. The poem's lines, "Yes I have committed acts of indecency with women/and most of them were acts of omission. I regret them/bitterly," especially left an impression on Rich, inciting her to consider how the silence and invisibility of lesbians rendered them powerless. The words made a heavy impact on Rich, who painfully recognized this silence in literature and in society, and in her own life. "Women's love for women has been presented almost entirely through silence and lies," she would later write in "Women and Honor: Some Notes on Lying" (*Adrienne Rich's Poetry and Prose* 190).

For the last few years, Rich had been committing herself politically and socially to women, and to now act upon her own lesbian desires seemed only natural. During the seventies, women calling themselves lesbian-feminists believed that the problems of the world stemmed from society's sexist attitudes toward women; in a way, lesbianism seemed like part of the solution to this patriarchy. In *Odd Girls and Twilight Lovers*, lesbian historian Lillian Faderman chronicles the emergence of lesbian-feminists who "came to believe that banding together could be effective only if a woman did not go home to sleep in the enemy camp but instead devoted all her energies—not only social and political but sexual as well—to other women" (Faderman 202). For some women, to be a lesbian-feminist was a political choice as much as it was a personal one. For example, the writer Rita Mae Brown, one of the earliest lesbian-feminists, proclaimed, "I became a lesbian because the culture that I live in is violently anti-woman. How could I, a woman, participate in a culture that denies my humanity? ... To give a man support and love before giving it to a sister is to support that culture, that power system" (Faderman 207).

Adrienne Rich had felt attraction toward women since she was a teenager, and now the "suppressed lesbian I had been carrying in me since adolescence began to stretch her limbs" (*Blood, Bread, and Poetry* 121). These early desires were heavily repressed until the Women's Movement gained power and offered new possibilities for love and partnership. Although Rich has also admitted that, at least during the seventies, sexual orientation was as much about political choice as it was about innate personal desires—"It wasn't as simple as falling in love—though falling in love always helps"—she has also made it clear that her lesbian desires were very much a part of her (O'Mahoney). "I identified myself as a radical feminist, and soon after—not as a political act but out of powerful and unmistakable feelings—as a lesbian," she stated in her foreword to *Blood, Bread, and Poetry* (viii).

Rich came out publicly as a lesbian in 1975, when she included "Re-Forming the Crystal" and "Phantasia for Elvira Shatayev" in the anthology *Amazon Poetry*. Edited by Joan Larkin and Elly Bulkin, the book includes such poets as Audre Lorde, May Sarton, Robin Becker, and Judy Grahn. The preface states that all of the poems "were written by women who define themselves as lesbians. And who have chosen, by publishing their poetry here, to affirm publicly that identity." Once Rich publicly disclosed her sexuality, she began openly identifying as a radical lesbian-feminist, an identity which informed her politics, her personal life, and her poetry. As she began to be more vocal about her lesbian identity and active in lesbian politics, it was obvious that her lesbianism meant more than just a switch in sexual partners. By committing herself politically and sexually to women, Rich became a spokesperson for feminists and lesbians.

Although Rich was active in many levels of the Women's Movement, her voice was most needed within the sacred walls of academia. As a member of the elite academic world, Rich spoke out against its inherent sexism, racism, and homophobia.

Rich was a key voice in questioning the authenticity of the Western Canon and critiquing the overall structure of the university. She was one of the earliest supporters of and influences on the development of women's studies classes and programs, which did not exist at any college in America before the late sixties.

A year after the publication of her two poems in *Amazon Poetry*, in December, 1976, Rich spoke at the Modern Language Association (MLA), an academic conference for English and literature studies, on a panel convened by the Women's Commission and Gay Caucus. Her co-panelists included the feminist writers June Jordan, Audre Lorde, and Honor Moore. In front of a large audience of teachers and scholars, Rich presented her essay, "It Is the Lesbian in Us," in which she linked lesbianism to creativity:

"And I believe it is the lesbian in every woman who is compelled by female energy, who gravitates toward strong women, who seeks a literature that will express that energy and strength. It is the lesbian in us who drives us to feel imaginatively, render in language, grasp the full connection between women and women. It is the lesbian in us who is creative ..." (*On Lies, Secrets, and Silence* 201).

The presentation, which caused a stir for the mostly heterosexual audience, offered the lesbians a representative voice.

Coming out as a lesbian affected Rich's life in a myriad of ways, not the least of which was becoming romantically involved with women. Intensely private about her personal life, Rich has remained fairly reticent concerning her early lesbian relationships, revealing only that her first "full-fledged act was to fall in love with a Jewish woman" (*Blood, Bread, and Poetry* 121). Then in 1976, Rich fell in love with the Jamaican-born novelist Michelle Cliff, who was then a copy editor working for Rich's publisher W.W. Norton. Rich was forty-seven years old and a mother of three; Cliff was thirty years old and had just begun to write fiction. The two began a romance that turned into a life-long relationship.

Cliff was born in Kingston, Jamaica, in 1946 and raised in the United States. She attended school in New York City, then completed a Ph.D. on the Italian Renaissance at the Warburg Institute at the University of London. When Rich met Cliff, she had just come back from London. Like Rich, Cliff was extremely active in the Women's Liberation Movement, and also devotee of the written word and language. She published her first book in 1980, and in the years since, has published several novels and short story collections. Her *No Telephone to Heaven* and *Bodies of Water* often appear on "post-colonialist" reading lists. Her fiction, which often takes place in Jamaica, explores colonialism and the issues of passing, disrupting, and blurring boundaries of race, class, gender, and sexuality. Considering herself a "white Creole," Cliff feels drawn to issues of hybridity and identity, and her characters often live between boundaries and categories. Cliff and Rich shared many of the same preoccupations with race, ethnicity, and lesbian identity, which perhaps initially drew them together. Although the two have been partners for nearly thirty years, Rich is unwilling to give any details of their relationship. "Michelle's a very private person," she says. "We keep our lives very separate, in terms of what our work is about, and deliberately so" (O'Mahoney).

By the mid-seventies, Rich's life had changed dramatically— she was now an outspoken member of the lesbian-feminist community, she had fallen in love with a woman who would become her lifelong partner, and her poetry was well known in the national literary community as well as among women-centered communities all over America. In addition to her poems, she had been publishing essays in small, feminist journals over the years, and in 1976, the same year Rich met Cliff, she published her first book of prose.

When *Of Woman Born: Motherhood as Experience and Institution,* Rich's first book of nonfiction, was published, it created a commotion among the critics which initiated the controversy that surrounds Rich's name. Part autobiography, history, and anthropology, *Of Woman Born* alienated some readers with its frank political overtones and its dissection of the institution of motherhood. For many women across America, however, the book was a revelation and a comfort.

Writing this book allowed Rich to finally be forthright about her struggles with motherhood, to write about "taboo" subjects; it also inspired her to re-connect, at least metaphorically, with all the women in her life. She dedicated the book to her grandmothers, Mary Gravely and Hattie Rice, and in the Acknowledgements, she expresses gratitude for the support of her mother and sister: "Finally, I cannot imagine having written this book without the presence in my life of my mother, who offers a continuing example of transformation and rebirth; and of my sister, with and from whom I go on learning about sisterhood, daughterhood, motherhood, and the struggle of women toward a shared, irreversible, liberation."

In *Of Woman Born,* which took Rich four years to write, she recalls her emotionally troubling time as a young mother, how she had often felt resentful and angry. The book also examines the mythic and anthropological history of motherhood, with Rich juxtaposing Western culture with cultures that honor female power; the complexity of mother-daughter bonds; and the domination of the birth process by male physicians—all important feminist concerns in the 1970s. Although Rich has often been stereotyped as a "man-hater," her position is much more complex. In *Of Woman Born,* instead of "bashing" men,

Rich was attempting to critique masculine culture and to celebrate the strength of women:

> We need to imagine a world in which every woman is the presiding genius of her own body. In such a world women will truly create new life, bring forth not only children (if and as we choose) but the visions, and the thinking, necessary to sustain, console, and alter human existence—a new relationship to the universe.... Sexuality, politics, intelligence, power, motherhood, word, community, intimacy will develop new meanings; thinking itself will be transformed. (*Of Woman Born*, 285–86)

In examining the stifling Westernized institution of motherhood, Rich envisions a new world, exalting autonomy for all women, regardless of race, class, sexuality, or nationality.

Although a success to many feminists, the book failed to impress mainstream critics. One of the earliest, and most damaging, reviews was by Helen Vendler in the *New York Review of Books,* in which Vendler, formally a fan of Rich's work, lambasted what she called Rich's "rhetoric of violence." Following this scathing review's lead, other major publications followed suit. According to the critic Kathleen Barry, as a result of this initial and fiery criticism, the book was basically censored: "Many bookstores that would have ordered the book did not do so. And the airwaves were silent—several major TV talk shows interviews which had been arranged by the publisher were cancelled" (Cooper 300).

Newspaper and magazine critics who had never paid attention to Rich's poetry were suddenly in full force, attacking Rich's feminist politics in sexist reviews that had nothing to do with the literary merit of the book. "This book is an absolute, radical witchery," wrote Alexander Theroux in *Boston Magazine* (Cooper

304). Theroux vehemently accused Rich as writing "in hysteria, in hate, and in hyperbole," (306), and then finally dismissed Rich's effort as some kind of "nervous breakdown" (307).

Rich was surprised by the viciousness of attacks on *Of Woman Born*. "There's no sense in pretending that critical opinion doesn't affect you, it does affect you," she admitted to Elly Bulkin. "Even when you are determined to go on with what you have to do. In a sense it can make you more tenacious of what you are about, it makes you know what you will and will not do, in a clearer way" (Bulkin 52).

The obvious homophobia behind many of the attacks was an awakening for Rich. She was called "man-hater" and dismissed as a hysterical radical lesbian. However, despite how painful these personal attacks were, they didn't sway Rich's social-political convictions; instead, the negative words reaffirmed for her that she must continue to write what she believed in and that she must remain visible—as a feminist, as a lesbian.

eight

Who is a Lesbian?

If I could let you know—
two women together is a work
nothing in civilization has made simple
                    —Adrienne Rich, "Twenty-One Love Poems"

AFTER WITNESSING OTHER MINORITY groups fight for justice, gays and lesbians rose to the occasion to make their own voices heard among the cries for liberation during the late sixties and seventies. The Gay Liberation Movement, like the Women's Movement, had been gaining power, as first seen in the Stonewall Riots of 1969, when drag queens, gay men, and a few lesbians fought back against the police in New York City. Unlike the McCarthy era of the 1950s, when gays and lesbians were closeted and fearful, many came together in the 1970s to fight against discrimination and homophobia. Activist groups, nightclubs, and organizations sprung up in the cities, and more and more people began to come out of the closet. For the first time, gays and lesbians achieved national visibility. Of course, this visibility also invited backlash, as seen with the entertainer and Christian fundamentalist Anita Bryant, who established the antigay Save Our Children Organization. In Dade, Florida, Bryant succeeded in convincing the citizens to repeal a new ordinance that prohibited discrimination against gays and lesbians in housing and employment. However, gay men and lesbians pulled together to protest Bryant, and to establish their battle for justice, which continues even now with the controversy over gay and lesbian marriage.

Although lesbian-feminists worked with gay men in protesting Bryant, many of them did not usually align themselves with the Gay Liberation Movement, which they felt was dominated by men who lacked understanding about women's issues and who supported the basic patriarchal structure. Their slogan became: "We are angry, not gay" (Faderman 211). Many lesbian-feminists felt that gay men were not concerned about the important political issues, and that they were more interested in the bar culture and bath houses than in changing the structure of society: "They complained that gay reformists pursued solutions that made no basic changes in the system that oppressed lesbians as women and their reforms would keep power in the hands of the oppressors" (Faderman 211).

At the 1977 New York Lesbian Pride Rally, an event which had split off from the Gay Pride Rally, Adrienne Rich spoke about these issues to a small crowd of women demonstrators. The Gay Pride Rally had focused on its anger toward Bryant, and Rich and other lesbian-feminists felt uncomfortable with the woman-hating tone of the march. In her speech, titled "The Meaning of Our Love for Women Is What We Have Constantly to Expand," Rich delineated how the lesbian-feminist movement was different from the gay male movement. "Much as the male homophobe hates the male homosexual, there is a far deeper—and extremely well-founded—dread in patriarchy of the mere existence of lesbians. Along with persecution, we have met with utter, suffocating silence and denial: the attempt to wipe us out of history and culture altogether," she proclaimed (*On Lies, Secrets, and Silence* 224). She pointed out that lesbians did not have the economic or cultural power of homosexual men, and that the workings of patriarchal American society and the gulf of silence surrounding female desire threatened lesbians in ways that gay men had not experienced. Rich blamed the influence of gay male culture, including "the violent, self-destructive world of the gay bars," and "the imitation role-stereotypes of 'butch' and 'femme'" for undermining the success of the gay liberation movement (225). Rich promoted instead what she saw as a new society, which consisted of a self-defined, women-identified culture: "I believe that a militant and pluralistic lesbian/feminist movement is potentially the greatest force in the world today for a complete transformation of society and of our relation to all life" (226).

Although Rich identified as a radical-lesbian, she never became a lesbian separatist, a movement which was growing in popularity. She did, however, sympathize with the movement.

Feminists vs. Lesbian-Feminists

When the Women's Movement began, the word "lesbian" was virtually absent from the rhetoric. It was not until late 1969 that radical feminists began to raise the issue of lesbian sexuality and visibility. When Betty Friedan, the leader of NOW, the largest organization of the women's movement, referred to lesbianism as "the lavender menace," warning it could undermine the credibility of the Women's Movement, she angered many lesbians and set off a growing divisiveness.

The issue exploded on May 1, 1970, at the second Congress to Unite Women, when members of Radicalesbians, wearing T-shirts that said "Lavender Menace," overtook the stage. For two hours, the protestors held the floor and talked about what it was like to be a lesbian in a heterosexist culture.

Although the controversy of lesbianism within the Women's Movement continued to flourish, the debates and differences didn't weaken the Women's Movement, as Friedan had feared. In fact, there were several moments of reconciliation and mutual support.

For instance, in 1970, when *Time* magazine ran a short piece that revealed that feminist leader Kate Millet was bisexual, feminists including Gloria Steinem and Susan Brownmiller held a press conference and surprised the press by declaring that women's liberation and gay liberation were working toward the same goals.

Then, in 1977, at the First National Women's Conference, which drew 20,000 representatives from all over the U.S., women gathered to draft and pass a National Plan of Action. When the question of lesbianism came up, to everyone's surprise, Betty Friedan supported the resolution to eliminate discrimination based on sexual orientation and preference. When the action passed, lesbian activists shouted, "Thank you, sisters," and released hundreds of pink and yellow balloons into the air that said "We Are Everywhere."

She had witnessed how the New Left had refused to support feminism, how the Gay Liberation Movement focused almost solely on homosexual men, and how some heterosexual feminists refused to acknowledge or support lesbians; however, despite all of the exclusion and homophobia, she believed that separating from mainstream society would only hurt the battle for equality and justice. Supporters of "dyke separatism" believed "that to withdraw from the immense, burgeoning diversity of the global women's movement will somehow provide a kind of purity and energy that will advance our freedom" (*On Lies, Secrets, and Silence* 227). However, Rich, whose three sons were an essential part of her life, felt that this was a simplistic idea. "Many times I have touched the edge of that pain and rage, and comprehended the impulse to dyke separation," she admitted. "But I believe it is a temptation into sterile 'correctness,' into powerlessness, an escape from radical complexity" (227). For Rich, the Women's Liberation Movement, in all of its forms and shapes, was the only hope. She believed it would only harm the movement to divide the issues between gay and straight. Women from all backgrounds must work together to dismantle patriarchy, to end racism and poverty, and to secure abortion rights, she explained, but then added that without the support of lesbians, the Women's Movement would never have existed: "[I]n this country, as in the world today, there is a movement of women going on like no other in history," she announced. "Let us have no doubt: it is being fueled and empowered by the work of lesbians" (228).

Both Rich's speeches and her prose reflected her fierce commitment to the Women's Movement and her identity as a lesbian-feminist, yet the majority of her poems, up until now, had made no explicit reference to her sexuality. Then in 1978, she published *The Dream of a Common Language*, another landmark book in Rich's career, which spoke to lesbians across America and "outed" Rich to the literary world.

Surprisingly, even with the lesbian content, the book found success with both critics and the public. In a review published in *Harper's*, Hayden Carruth, Rich's cast-off old friend, commented on Rich's notorious politics and polemical writing, and claimed that these poems rose above the ongoing controversy:

> The new poems spring from the same locus of thought and feeling that has generated Rich's recent polemical writing, particularly her book *Of Woman Born*, which has stimulated so much discussion since it appeared a couple of years ago. But whereas I found in the polemic minor points of irrationality, even hysteria, that rather spoiled the whole effect, the poems are firm, assured, calm. (Cooper 271)

At their best, Rich's poems, although political, avoid becoming mired in ideology, and instead ask probing, difficult questions, while at the same time moving the reader with their beauty, language, and depth. "I don't know if Rich's radical feminist ideology contains mechanisms that might be made to account for this difference between her prose and poetry, and in the present discussion I don't care," added Carruth. "What is important is that Rich is a poet, a genuine poet, and has been all her life" (Cooper 271).

Rich's feminist convictions are certainly recognizable in the poetry of *Dreams*. Some of the poems collected in the book include historical monologue and portraits, as in "Paula Becker to Clara Westhoff," in which Rich imagines the relationship between the two women, one of whom was the wife of Rainer Maria Rilke. In the poem "Hunger," dedicated to her friend, the poet Audre Lorde, Rich imagines what it would be like if a community of women worked together to transform society:

"Until we find each other, we are alone." No longer does Rich proclaim that androgyny is the way to find wholeness, as she did in "Diving into the Wreck," when she wrote, "I am she: I am he." Now Rich focuses on what it means to be a woman, exploring how women need to rely on each other in order to resist and survive. "I don't think of androgyny as progress anymore, I think it's a useless term," she told Elly Bulkin. "It's essentially the notion that the male will somehow incorporate into himself female attributes—tenderness, gentleness, ability to cry, to feel, to express, not to be rigid" (Bulkin 62).

What *Dreams* is best known for is the group of lesbian sonnets that fall at the center of the book. These "Twenty-One Love Poems" were originally published by a small feminist house, Effie's Press, as a separate booklet, which the writer Olga Broumas, in her review of *Dreams*, recalled as a publication that "one thousand of us have jealously owned, and a great many more have read, in its beautiful, small editing from Effie's Press" (Cooper 277).

"Twenty-One Love Poems" follows in the tradition of Petrarch's love poems and Shakespeare's sonnets, in that the speaker of the poem is talking to a beloved, and the voice is romantic, intimate, and passionate. However, as Rich explains, "This is something different, a female and lesbian sensuality and sensibility that has not been in poetry before" (*Adrienne Rich's Poetry and Prose* 271). The poems are not only love poems, but also critiques of patriarchal notions of love as well as affirmations of love between women. "No one has imagined us," writes Rich, describing a lesbian relationship, her words giving visibility to what historically had been so closeted in both literature and society. "Two women who are lovers in heterosexist society live with contradictions embedded in their most intimate thoughts and feelings," observes the feminist writer Adrian Oktenberg. "What they experience as beautiful, and as absolutely natural, the rest of society views as ugly and perverted" (Cooper 77).

These poems also allow the reader a rare glimpse into Rich's personal love life, as she writes clearly of her erotic relationship with another woman. The poems are both a celebration of their love, and also a testament to the difficulty of their lives.

> ... You've kissed my hair
> to wake me. *I dreamed you were a poem,*
> I say, *a poem I wanted to show someone ...*
> and I laugh and fall dreaming again
> of the desire to show you to everyone I love,
> to move openly together
> in the pull of gravity, which is not simple

Writing such poems, especially after the homophobic reactions to *Of Woman Born*, risked condemnation from homophobic critics; however, Rich refused to live or to write from the closet any longer. In commenting on the love poems, Rich explained to Elly Bulkin that she wanted to show how the lovers existed in relation to the larger world, to expose the way the private is always wedded to the public: "You're never just in bed together in a private space; you can't be, there is a hostile and envious world out there, acutely threatened by women's love for each other" (Bulkin 57).

Deeply committed to her hope for a women-led society, Rich later explained that she wrote these poems intended for a lesbian audience. When she discovered that other people, men and heterosexuals, were re-interpreting the poems, she felt troubled:

> Two friends of mine, both artists, wrote me about reading
> the *Twenty-One Love Poems* with their male lovers, assuring

me how 'universal' the poems were. I found myself angered, and when I asked myself why, I realized that it was anger at having my work essentially assimilated and stripped of its meaning, 'integrated' into heterosexual romance. That kind of 'acceptance' of the book seems to me a refusal of its deepest implications.... I see that as a denial, a kind of resistance, a refusal to read and hear what I've actually written, to acknowledge what I am. (Bulkin, "Part II" 58)

Rich felt as if she were being misunderstood and interpreted wrongly, and essentially told her readers to understand the identity politics clearly explained in her prose before they made any attempt to read her poetry. "We're not trying to become part of the old order misnamed 'universal' which has tabooed us; we are transforming the meaning of 'universality,'" she added (58).

During this period of her life, some readers and critics felt alienated by Rich's radical politics, but Rich no longer felt sensitive to mainstream criticism. She instead focused her energy on feminist and lesbian issues, and aligned herself with those who were on the margins of American society. Rich increasingly drew large crowds (often consisting entirely of women) to her readings, and her popularity as a poet and feminist rose.

Rich's next published book of prose, *On Lies, Secrets, and Silence: Selected Prose 1966–1978,* maps out her feminist-lesbian ideology and political alliances in twenty-two essays, most of which were originally published in small feminist journals. These essays cover a wide range of topics, including literary commentary on Jane Eyre, Anne Bradstreet, and Emily Dickinson; critical examinations of patriarchal institutions, including universities; and brilliant explorations of lesbian and feminist politics.

Rich soon rose as one of the more prominent intellectuals in the women's movement, admired for her poetry, her passionate speaking, and her precise, eloquent prose. "Feminism means finally that we renounce our obedience to the fathers and recognize the world they have described is not the whole world," she wrote in "Conditions for Work." "Feminism implies that we recognize fully the inadequacy for us, the distortion, of male-created ideologies, and that we proceed to think and act, out of that recognition" (*On Lies, Secrets, and Silence* 207). Although she viewed feminism through the critical lens of an intellectual, she was never out of touch with the community of women as a whole, including women of color, lesbians, and working class women; Rich never locked herself up in an ivory tower, but was very much a part of her surroundings.

Rich believed that a women-centered community, which she explains must include *all* women, was the only way to change patriarchal society. She hoped that feminists could overcome the issues that were beginning to threaten the movement from within, including racism, elitism, and homophobia. Many women of color felt as if they did not have a voice in the Women's Movement, which often seemed mired in the issues of white, middle-upper-class women.

Rich listened closely to the criticisms of these women, and in doing so, expanded her understanding of the Women's Movement. Since the 1960s, Rich had been educating herself in issues of racism and classism, beginning with the work of James Baldwin and developing into her involvement in the Civil Rights Movement. The Black Panthers had taught her about radicalism, and many of her ideas about feminism were shaped by black feminists. Toni Cade Bambara's *The Black Woman* (1970), Michele Russell's "An Open Letter to the Academy" (1981), and Barbara Smith's essay "Toward a Black Feminist Criticism" all troubled and inspired Rich, encouraging her to closely examine the "whiteness" of feminism.

Rich was close friends with many prominent lesbian-feminists during the time, including the radical-lesbian Mary Daly, author of *Gyn/Ecology* (1978), and the lesbian-feminist Audre Lorde, whom Rich called "one of the most sensual and sensuous woman poets I can think of" (*Adrienne Rich's Poetry and Prose* 271). As women tried to define themselves and a movement, there were many debates and open dialogues among them, often in the form of essays or letters published in feminist journals. For example, when Daly overlooked issues of race and diversity in her work, Rich criticized her in an essay, "Notes for a Magazine: What does Separatism Mean?," in which Rich commented, "surely not all differences are terrifying" (Yorke 84). Audre Lorde also criticized Daly, and spoke out about the way she, as a black lesbian, felt left out of the Women's Movement. Black feminists influenced Rich's thinking about sexuality, race, and power; Yorke points out that early in the movement, Rich aligned "her position with newly emergent Black feminist groups which had as their aim the formation of a broader-based political movement" (Yorke 83). Rich was known for her thoughtfulness and her conscientious manner. She was not easily swayed, but would closely study the various arguments and dialogues about sexuality and race. In an interview with Audre Lorde, author of *Coal* and *The Black Unicorn,* Rich admitted much of what Lorde said about racism was difficult to come to terms with, as a white woman: "So it's not that I can just accept your perceptions unblinkingly. Some of them are very hard for me. But I don't want to deny them. I know I can't afford to" (Yorke 85).

Rich increasingly identified with women who felt they were being marginalized within the Women's Movement itself, whether by race, class, or sexuality, and she began to feel distanced from some of the women who had once been her allies. In addition to politics of race, issues between heterosexual feminists and lesbian feminists began to cause tensions within the movement, which for Rich came to a breaking point in 1979, at a Women Against Porn (WAP) conference. During a panel discussion, a "heckler" in the crowd, a woman wearing a man's suit, accused the speakers of being elitist. One of the panelists, Susan Brownmiller, a prominent feminist and journalist, responded: "If you hate men so much, why are you wearing men's clothes?" (*In Our Time* 309). Her careless remark incited heated argument and emotional outpouring among the panelists and attendees. A few days later, Adrienne Rich, out of support for the lesbians at the conference, resigned from WAP, citing Brownmiller's "homophobic attack on a lesbian wearing pants" (310).

The two women had worked together for years, and for Brownmiller, Rich's resignation was a stinging loss. She immediately tried to call Rich on the phone to discuss what had happened, but Rich, known for her stubbornness, refused to talk to Brownmiller. In her memoir of the Women's Movement, Brownmiller recalled what was to be the end of their friendship:

> When I called her home in Western Massachusetts she would not hear me out. Adrienne and I had been political allies for nearly a decade, and I treasured the company of this brilliant, internationally recognized poet who bore up so stoically under physical disability and personal trauma, whose twin worlds of intellectual achievement and radical activism were an unending search for perfection. We never spoke again. (310)

Rich detests all forms of homophobia, misogyny, racism, or classism, and in her eyes, Brownmiller had crossed the line. Although Rich is known to be stubborn and difficult, and sometimes her strong stances on issues can seem tenacious, her friends and supporters also speak of her integrity, courage, and honesty. In this case, Rich felt that she could not associate with someone who was homophobic.

Until this point, most of Rich's essays illustrated her views on radical-feminism and emphasized the importance of communities of women working together to dismantle patriarchal structures. Although she had written a few essays on lesbian identity, it had not been her central focus. Then, in 1980, she published an essay that would question many of the common assumptions about lesbians and heterosexual women.

"Compulsory Heterosexuality and Lesbian Existence," one of Rich's most important, ground-breaking essays, appeared in the scholarly feminist journal *Signs* in the summer of 1980, following a request for a special "sexuality" issue. Immediately on its publication, the essay provoked intense discussion and debate in the women's movement. It is probably still her most controversial theoretical essay. Rich's intentions were to: "challenge the erasure of lesbian existence from so much of scholarly feminist literature"; "encourage heterosexual feminists to examine heterosexuality as a political institution which disempowers women"; reclaim the word "lesbian"; and broaden the meaning of lesbianism (*Blood, Bread, and Poetry* 23).

In the essay Rich challenges society's definition of lesbians as deviant or perverse, and she also radically critiques what she terms "institutionalized heterosexuality," which "strips women of their autonomy, dignity and sexual potential, including the potential of loving and being loved by women in mutuality and integrity" (*Blood, Bread, and Poetry* 24). She argues that women have had little choice about their relationships with men, and that heterosexuality is compulsory and enforced by all means possible. She also wants to rid lesbianism of its sex-only meaning and remove lesbianism from the realm of the exotic.

Instead of "lesbianism," Rich proposes "lesbian existence" and "lesbian continuum."

> *Lesbian existence* suggests both the fact of the historical presence of lesbians and our continuing creation of the meaning of that existence. I mean the term *lesbian continuum* to include a range—through each woman's life and throughout history—of woman-identified experience, not simply the face that a woman has had or consciously desired genital sexual experience with another woman. (*Blood, Bread, and Poetry* 51)

One of the more controversial ideas in the essay is the idea of a "lesbian continuum," in which, according to the critic Liz Yorke, Rich "attempts to collapse the difference, that is, the dualistic dichotomy—between heterosexual and lesbian women" (Yorke 78). The basic idea of the lesbian continuum is that a woman does not have to engage in sex with another woman in order to be considered a lesbian, and that lesbian is a broad enough category to include all types of connections between women. Rich essentially proposes a scale, with lesbian at one end and heterosexuality at the other, and suggest that most women fall somewhere in the middle. Many theorists and critics objected to this definition for ignoring the experiences of lesbians who have come out of the closet, who have faced persecution and prejudice. The feminist scholar Gloria Bowles asks, "If we make all female love part of the 'lesbian continuum,' then what do we call the experience of women who have come out and suffered enormously for doing so?" (Cooper 322).

In a letter to the editors of *Signs*, Rich expressed her frustration with the way the essay had been received: "What I had thought to delineate rather complexly as a continuum has begun to sound more like 'life-style shopping'," she complained. Despite the controversy, Rich's essay had a profound effect on feminism, lesbianism, and gender studies. Although some feminist critics would later criticize Rich for what many saw as an "essentialist" argument and "identity politics," other critics have risen to her defense. The critic Liz Yorke, for one, argues that despite the question of "identity politics" Rich's influence on feminism and queer studies is indisputable, and that "Compulsory Heterosexuality" "was clearly an impulse towards creating bridges between women—but it is rarely praised for its major contribution in providing lesbian and gay theory with a powerful critique of heterosexuality as an institution" (Yorke 18).

Many feminists have regarded Rich as a prominent theorist as much as a poet, and also as a scholar who helped change the face of women's studies programs by contributing radical ideas to theoretical debates in gender and women studies. From 1981 to 1983, Rich co-edited the lesbian/feminist journal *Sinister Wisdom* with her partner Michelle Cliff (the two had left New York City in 1979 and were now living in Massachusetts). In the first issue, they co-wrote an introduction, espousing their belief in the intellectual aspect of feminism.

We believe that many more women should be writing theory.... Unfortunately, when we explore our concrete experiences without theory-making, we are left *with* isolated instances, feelings of victimization, therapy insights, perhaps, but no sense of how these experiences belong to a larger whole, or how we can move out from them not just as individuals but with large numbers of other women.

Theory was as important to the movement as direct activism, and it was crucial, they argued, not to have one without the other.

Although Rich contributed to the field of feminist theory with her essays and her tireless promotion of lesbian-feminist principles, she always viewed herself primarily as a poet. In her next book, *A Wild Patience Has Taken Me This Far: Poems, 1978–1981,* her poetry continued to celebrate the accomplishments of women and to reclaim women whose lives had been erased from history or been distorted. There are portraits of Willa Cather, Simone Weil, and Ethel Rosenberg, and also on friendship between women, including Susan B. Anthony and Elizabeth Cady Stanton, and Emily and Charlotte Brontë. "History has always felt to me an immense resource for art, and poetry as a place where history can be kept alive—not grand master narratives, but otherwise forgotten or erased people and actions," Rich told interviewer Rachel Spence (*Arts of The Possible* 141). These poems also include references to Rich's personal life, which are woven in with the historical and political. In the poem, "Mother-In-Law," Rich speaks about her husband's death and claims her own identity: "Your son is dead/ten years, I am a lesbian,/my children are themselves." After almost fifteen years of virtual silence on the death of her husband, Rich began to write her way through the grief, betrayal, and sadness, composing one of her most autobiographical poems and re-exploring the complexity of her Jewish background.

■ chapter
nine

Moving Beyond the Personal

The faithful drudging child
the child at the oak desk whose penmanship,
hard work, style will win her prizes
becomes the woman with a mission, not to win prizes
but to change the laws of history.

—Adrienne Rich, "Sources"

IN THE 1980s, RICH BEGAN to re-explore her Jewish heritage in the long poem "Sources" and the personal essay "Split at the Root." Rich, who has always felt "split," as "neither gentile nor Jew," considers how her father and her husband may have contributed to her feelings of displacement. Both men haunted Rich throughout adulthood, and in order to reach some kind of peace with them, she felt she had to write about them. Although her father was already present in her work, Rich felt she had to return to him once again: "I have to claim my father, for I have my Jewishness from him and not from my gentile mother; and I have to break his silence, his taboos; in order to claim him I have in a sense to expose him ... I have to face the sources and the flickering presence of my own ambivalence as a Jew" (*Blood, Bread, and Poetry* 100).

Rich completed "Sources," a twenty-three-part poem that is one of the most probing of her autobiographical and cultural explorations, in 1982. In this poem, which appears in *Your Native Land, Your Life: Poems* (1986), Rich examines how the two men, both dead, shaped her life as a woman and a poet. Rich portrays her father as stern, authoritative, and her husband as intensely private, brooding. Although Rich does not excuse their actions and their emotional distance, she addresses them with honesty and tenderness. "[T]here is compassion and love for these men who have been damaged by the patriarchal equation of masculinity with invulnerability, as well as by anti-Semitism itself," suggests Wendy Martin. "Driven by the injunction to be self-sufficient and independent, both men cut themselves off from the past, from the sources of emotion and identity that might have sustained them" (Martin 226). Rich implies that if her father and husband had recognized and connected to their roots, perhaps they would have been more whole, more emotionally available.

Much of the poem focuses on Rich's father and the influence

he had over her life and examines the dialogue that began in childhood and continued into the present. "For years I struggled with you: your categories, your theories,/your will, the cruelty which came inextricable from your love. For/years all arguments I carried on in my head were with you." Rich holds up a magnifying glass to their relationship, revealing at once the suffocation and the intimacy she endured. In order to find freedom, she had to rebel, she had to shake herself free from his words: "I saw myself, the/eldest daughter raised as a son, taught to study but not to pray, taught to/hold reading and writing sacred: the eldest daughter in a house with no son, she who must overthrow the father, take what he taught her and/ use it against him." For so long, she could only see her father as the family patriarch, demanding, controlling, and rigid, and it was difficult for her to "see beneath it the suffering of the Jew, the alien stamp you bore, because/you had deliberately arranged that it should be invisible to me. It is/only now, under a powerful, womanly lens, that I can decipher your/suffering and deny no part of my own."

When she writes about her husband, whom her father did not want her to marry because of the "wrong accent, the wrong class," Rich realizes that he had more in common with her father than she had ever considered. Both men suffered because of their denial of their roots; both, in different ways, tried to suppress their pasts. When Rich addresses her husband, she is careful, tender. She admits it has been difficult for her to write about him, as she did not want him to be reduced to merely a poetic subject. For years she had been "protecting your existence"; yet now her desire to make some kind of peace with him overpowers her reservation: "I can't finish this without speaking to you."

Over the years, Rich's identity has splintered in many directions. "Sometimes I feel I have seen too long from too many disconnected angles: white, Jewish, anti-Semite, racist, anti-racist, once-married, lesbian, middle-class, feminist, exmatriate southerner, *split at the root*—that I will never bring them whole," she professes (*Blood, Bread, and Poetry* 122). It is this sort of honesty that has driven Rich's work and connected her to her audience. Over the years, she has endeavored to know herself, to heal these split roots; yet for Rich, this has never meant retreating from the world. Whether teaching remedial English classes at a city college or speaking at lesbian rallies, Rich has always been a part of what surrounds her. What Rich wants, she explains in "Sources" is "an end to suffering," but she argues that this is not "anesthesia." It is not retreating, closing oneself off; instead, to find peace, "I mean knowing the world/and my place in it."

Throughout her life, Rich has remained open and flexible, finding new places in the world, and never opposing change. During the sixties, when Rich moved from Cambridge to New York City, her life opened in new ways. In 1984, the setting of Rich's life changed again, when she and Cliff uprooted from their East Coast home to move 3,000 miles to Santa Cruz, California, where they currently live. Rich, who had been teaching at Cornell, was offered a position as Distinguished Visiting Professor at San Jose State University. The setting was quite a change from the urban streets of New York and the quiet New England setting of Massachusetts. Now they made their home on a stretch of Pacific coastline surrounded by palms and guava trees, a stunning landscape which would begin to appear in Rich's poems.

Similarly, the political landscape in America also began to shift. The 1980s was a decade overshadowed by Reagan's politics, corporate power, conservatism, the arms race, a growing split between the wealthy and poor, and the AIDS epidemic. During these years Rich committed herself to battling for social

The AIDS Epidemic

The AIDS epidemic transformed the gay and lesbian community. The first cases of AIDS, which were then diagnosed as a rare cancer, were reported in 1981. Soon it seemed as if gay men everywhere were being diagnosed with this deadly disease. The gay community quickly mobilized, creating crucial organizations such as the Gay Men's Health Crisis in New York City, to provide services and assistance.

As personal and social tragedy increased to startling, immense proportions, AIDS also strengthened the political aim of the Gay Movement. AIDS made political activism and mobilization a matter of life and death.

In the early years of the epidemic, AIDS was rarely discussed in the national media or by political officials, but as the numbers of infected gay men increased, the epidemic helped fuel and intensify the antigay rhetoric of the New Right. Several public officials called for coercive public health policies, including mandatory HIV testing and quarantines. In angry response, various activist groups formed, including the radical ACT-UP (AIDS Coalition To Unleash Power). ACT-UP used direct-action and confrontational tactics to fight against the AIDS epidemic, promote awareness of AIDS, and challenge the indifference of politicians and government officials who had not responded adequately to the crisis.

AIDS also led to a crucial reconciliation between gay men and lesbians, as many lesbians felt called upon to take an active role in helping care for the dying men. The result was tremendous political and social unity among gays and lesbians, as exemplified at the 1987 National March on Washington for Lesbian and Gay Rights, which drew approximately 650,000 participants, the largest civil rights march in American history.

justice, expanding her ideas about feminism, lesbianism, class, and race. She now found herself returning to the philosophy of Marx, recommitting herself as a socialist, and thinking about social justice on a more global level. She spoke out against all forms of violence, especially focusing on anti-Semitism, racism, and homophobia.

Although she was still deeply committed to feminism and justice for women, the scope of the Women's Liberation Movement began to shift for Rich in the eighties. Disenchanted with the way feminism seemed stuck in a white, middle-class perspective, Rich expanded her political activism to be more inclusive of other countries, nationalities, and cultures. She no longer used the word "feminism," but returned to the early phrase, "women's liberation," which she felt was broader and more inclusive. She urged American feminists to be more sensitive to the needs of women of color and varying economic classes, and she committed herself to reaching out to women from other countries and learning about their issues. For example, she met with many Latin American feminists in the early eighties, and then in July, 1985, she traveled to Nicaragua to study with the Sandinistas.

Nicaragua had elected Sandinista leader Daniel Ortega as president in 1984. His left-wing government was opposed by the U.S.-supported guerillas, the Contras. During the 1980s, the CIA financed, supplied, and supervised command raids with the Contras on the Sandinista government. Many liberals in the United States were appalled and angered by the U.S. government's attempt to dismantle what was apparently a democratically elected government. Rich's political alliances lay with the Sandinistas. After she attended the Conference on Central America, she documented this experience in her book of essays *Blood, Bread, and Poetry*: "Listening to and learning from the women and men dedicated to creating a new

Nicaraguan society felt more urgent, more necessary to my own feminist politics than pressing questions like abortion, which is still illegal there" (*Blood, Bread, and Poetry* 157). As Rich became more engaged in fighting for justice on a global, international level, she also revised earlier views about men, and now accepted that men and women could successfully govern together.

In the 1980s, Rich committed herself to various groups outside the mainstream. She joined progressive Jewish organizations such as Jews for Racial and Economic Justice, Jews Against Genocide, and the New Jewish Agenda. Although not a religious person, Rich wanted to re-claim her father's heritage and examine how Jewish history and culture has been patriarchal and misogynist. She was one of the founding members of the editorial group for the literary journal, *Bridges: A Journal for Jewish Feminists and Our Friends,* and she was also involved with other activists supporting peaceful solutions for Israel and Palestine.

Rich also involved herself in supporting the gay and lesbian community. During the 1980s, America's gay and lesbian community was deeply affected by the AIDS epidemic. Young men were dying at a rapid rate, and the government basically ignored the problem. The crisis brought many gay men and lesbians together, healing past differences. Rich's views toward the Gay Movement had changed since the 1970s when it had been difficult for her visualize lesbians and gay men working together because of the patriarchal presence of gay men. Now she witnessed an inclusion of women in the Gay Movement, and also saw how lesbians were stepping up to take care of men who were sick. "I think AIDS transformed a lot of gay men, and many lesbians came to the bedsides of their friends with AIDS," she told Michael Klein. "I think about the possibilities for empathy, for mutual solidarity among gay men and lesbians, not simply as people who suffer under homophobia, but as people who are also extremely creative, active, and have a particular understanding of the human condition." When one of her close friends and supporters, the literary critic David Kalstone, died of AIDS, Rich dedicated a poem to him: "Give me your living hand/If I could take the hour/death moved into you undeclared, unnamed/—even if sweet, if I could take that hour." As a lesbian poet who has been out of the closet since the seventies, Rich has undoubtedly been an important role model for many lesbian and gay writers. In her work, she continues to stress the importance of visibility.

Rich continued to publish books of poetry and to speak at a variety of engagements, securing her reputation as one of the country's most accomplished poets. From 1986 to 1993, she was Professor of English at Stanford University, straddling the worlds of academia and activism. Although some critics continued to denounce her work as didactic, others praised her for taking risks and for writing about significant issues. In 1989, she published *Time's Power: Poems 1985–1988,* which was followed by *An Atlas of the Difficult World: Poems 1988–1991.* In both books, Rich speaks chillingly of the violence and hate-crimes in America, and embraces those citizens who have been pushed to the margins of society "who are hated as being of our kind: faggot kicked into the icy/river, woman dragged from her stalled car/into the mist-struck mountains, used and hacked to death."

In contrast to the 1970s, when Rich had written her poetry for a woman or lesbian-only audience; she now broadened her audience to include all Americans, those disenchanted Americans who had been exploited, abused, violated, and let down by their country. "An Atlas of the Difficult World" is a long, complex poem, similar in style to those of political poets like Walt Whitman, Muriel Rukeyser, or Allen Ginsberg. In the poem, which is constructed in thirteen parts, Rich espouses the idea of knowing one's country, however painful and disappointing it may be.

In one of the poem's most harrowing sections, Rich writes about two lesbians who were shot when hiking the Appalachian Trail in Pennsylvania. The tragedy occurred on May 13, 1988, when Stephen Roy Carr shot Rebecca Wright and her lover Claudia Brenner. Rebecca was instantly killed, but Claudia survived five bullet wounds and managed to crawl away for help. During the legal proceedings, it became clear that Carr had attacked the women because they were lesbians.

> I don't want to know how he tracked them
> along the Appalachian Trail, hid close
> by their tent, pitched as they thought in seclusion
> killing one woman, the other
> dragging herself into town   his defense they had teased his
>   loathing
> of what they were   I don't want to know
>   "Atlas of the Difficult World"

Rich started writing the poem before the Gulf War and did not finish until after the war was over, and during this period of time, she felt alarmed and aggrieved by America's acts of violence. However, no matter how terrible and shocking the violence, Rich refused to look away, to pretend everything was fine. "I keep on not wanting to know what I know—Matthew Shepard, James Byrd Jr., the schoolyard massacres," she explained to Michael Klein. "There keep being things that I absolutely don't want to know, and must know—and we as a society must know." A poet is a witness to history, and, especially in Rich's case, a citizen who calls on her audience to question the world and then to take action.

The final section of the poem, "Dedications," reflects on the condition of America, and also addresses all of the people who may be reading the poem and searching for their place in the world. Rich explained to the journalist Bill Moyers that she wrote this section "very consciously as a citizen poet, looking at the geography, the history, the peoples of my country" (Moyers 345).

Throughout the nineties, Rich remained politically active and outspoken about her convictions, and published prose and poetry that further advocated her beliefs, including *What is Found There: Notebooks on Poetry and Politics* and *Dark Fields of the Republic: Poems 1991–1996*. During the decade, she was awarded numerous honors and awards, including the Robert Frost Silver Medal of the Poetry Society of America; the William Whitehead Award of the Publishing Triangle for lifetime achievement in letters; and the prestigious MacArthur "Genius Grant" Fellowship.

Rich's commitment to feminism, her convictions to put poetry, language, and government back into the hands of the people, her anti-elitism, and her battles against homophobia, racism, and classism, have been inspiring for many people; however, she has also angered traditional establishments and prominent figures. She was first the subject of dispute in 1996 when she edited *Best American Poetry;* the literary critic Harold Bloom, known for his defense of the Western Canon, criticized Rich for choosing poems that were, in his view, based on the authors' minority status more than on the quality of the poems. A year later, Rich entered the spotlight again when she declined the National Medal for the Arts, citing the hypocrisy of the U.S. government, which, she claimed, had selected a few token artists while threatening to dismantle support for the arts in America.

Through her writing, interviews, and participation in various readings and poetry festivals, Rich has spoken about her hope for a better world, and the changes needed for this to happen. Although she disagrees with many American government policies, she has not exiled herself to another country, as writers and artists have sometimes been known to do. Rich is not an expatriate. Instead she has chosen to live in America and to write about it, to expose all of its violence, contradictions, and freedoms. "This older Adrienne Rich courageously assumes that Americans can be trusted and encouraged to think, share common perceptions, and develop more national cooperation, focusing together on a higher vision of the republic and citizens' responsibilities to it," suggests the critic Cheri Colby Langdell. "She is most alive as a poet when exploring the ethical, spiritual, or political terrain and charting the atlas of this difficult land" (Langdell 226).

Rich often speaks out about her frustration with the way poetry is ignored in America and how it has been "hoarded inside the schools, inside the universities" (Rothschild). She also criticizes her contemporaries for not writing about political and social issues. As the poetry of the eighties and nineties grew more individualistic, a "huge retrenchment—not just in poetry—into the personal," Rich found herself writing against this trend, to offer ways of thinking in terms of social and collective values (da Costa). In contrast to her support for the early consciousness-raising groups of the Women's Movement, Rich rejected the idea of support and therapy groups in her later years.

One of the things I have to say about this demon of the personal—and I have to take responsibility for my part in helping create this demon, as part of a women's movement in which we celebrated personal experience and personal feelings—is that it has become a horribly commoditized version of humanity. It's almost as though the personal life has been taken hostage in some way, and I'm shying away more and more from anything that would contribute to that. (Klein)

Although Rich has been reluctant to speak about her personal life, pieces of her life continue to appear in her work. She continues to live in Santa Cruz with her partner Michelle Cliff, but does not usually talk about their relationship. "I feel there is something frankly sexist about probing my sexual life rather than discussing my work and my ideas. I think that it would not be done to a male poet and thinker" (O'Mahoney). She is now a grandmother, and despite early tensions of motherhood, she is quite close to her three sons. Rich once said, "If I could have one wish for my own sons, it is that they should have the courage of women" (*Of Woman Born* 215).

Rich has maintained a vigorous regimen of writing, readings, teachings, judging contests, and participating in political events; however, recently, she has slowed her activities, due to age and declining health. She has had numerous surgeries, including spinal surgery in 1992. The arthritis, that has plagued her since she was a young woman, makes it difficult for her to travel. She is fragile and stooped, using a cane to help her walk; at times the intense pain has nearly rendered her immobile.

However, whenever Rich gives a reading, the room is always packed. Rich's readings are not like traditional poetry readings, in which usually only other poets or college students attend. Rich's readings are gatherings of art and activism, a place where personal and political merge. She is known for her strong reading voice, the powerful way she emphasizes words and rhythms. Although she is tiny and now, at seventy-five, her hair is gray and her body is bent, she is an impressive presence on the stage. "In person, Rich is bright, engaging and instantly likeable, with a strain of unassailable independence in her voice," observed the journalist John O'Mahoney.

Rich entered the new century with a flurry of publishing and activity. She published *Midnight Salvage: Poems 1995–1998, The Arts of the Possible*, and *Fox: Poems 1998–2000*. She won the 2003 Yale Bollingen Prize for American Poetry, which carries a cash award of $50,000, in recognition of her lifetime achievement and the recent book *Fox*. The judges cited her "honesty, at once ferocious and humane, her deep learning, her continuous poetic exploration and awareness of multiple selves."

Rich has also continued to be politically active, supporting, for instance, the Clark Kissinger international campaign to free Mumia Abu-Jamal. Rich signed a letter, along with Michelle Cliff, Barbara Kingsolver, Grace Paley, and Susan Brownmiller, to protest Kissinger's and Mumia's imprisonment. She has also become involved in protesting the war in Iraq, attending anti-war activities and poetry readings. "It is exhilarating to be alive in a time of awakening of consciousness; it can also be confusing, disorienting, and painful," she said in the period after 9/11 and before the Iraq war (Langdell 223). Rich participated in the National Day of Poetry against the War, reading with poets that included W.S. Merwin and Stanley Kunitz, on the same day as Laura Bush's cancelled literary symposium on "Poetry and the American Voice."

Although writing can be a lonely act, Rich counts on the communities she is a part of to provide her with stimulation and support. "[T]he kinds of support and the kinds of challenge that I receive from the lives of others around me—poets, non-poets, and other kinds of artists, and activists—carries me," she told Bill Moyers. "I don't feel like a solitary person in my lonely room at all, even though I have to spend hours alone in a room to do what I do" (Moyers 348).

Urging other artists to move beyond their own lives to learn about others' experiences, Rich believes that people need to understand who they are as individuals, without secluding themselves in a personal vacuum: "With any personal history, what is to be done? What do we know when we know your story? *With whom do you believe your lot is cast?*" (*Arts of the Possible* 155). The best of Rich's work challenges her listeners to look and act beyond the boundaries of their own personal lives, and calls on artists and poets to be witnesses to the world:

> It seems to me that it is the responsibility of an artist to move out from our own necessarily circumscribed lives into the experience of others whom we don't know and might never know, and in doing this to experience what we could never have experienced ourselves. Being aware of the diverse lives around us and the conditions in which they are being lived is not just one way of making art. I think that it's also a responsibility and a source of strength. It's a tremendous resource. (Moyers 350)

ten

The Critical Response

For almost fifty years, Rich's fierce intelligence has been leading the way for generations of poets, challenging received ideals, changing lives, giving voice to the disenfranchised. Always, her effort has been to connect; to discover relationships between the tangled, fragmented peripheries of our inner lives and the seemingly unrelated events of history; to understand the interdependencies of our sexual and political lives; and, perhaps with renewed or more reconsidered focus in recent years, to achieve a voice that is at once both intensely personal and public.

—Carol Bere, "The Road Taken:
Adrienne Rich in the 1990s"

ONE OF THE COUNTRY'S MOST popular living poets, Adrienne Rich has produced a reputable body of work that has
spanned a fifty-year career and received some of America's most
distinguished poetry awards. She has also left lasting impressions on the field of women studies and political activism. Her
essays and feminist ideas appear in every women's studies program and her award-winning poetry is published in nearly
every major anthology of American poetry.

Over the past fifty years, Rich's work has attracted many supporters and fiery critics. Like no other poet today, Rich has
been critiqued as much for her politics as for the quality of her
poems. Despite the divisive opinions on her work, Rich has
remained wholly committed to the art of poetry, as well as to
her political convictions.

At the start of her career, Adrienne Rich was hailed by critics
as an impressive new voice in poetry. She won the esteemed
Yale Younger Poets Competition and received glowing praise
from W.H. Auden. She was one of the few women who
accepted into the circle of elite poets in the 1940s and 1950s.
When her second book also met favorable reviews, it seemed as
if Rich was on a clear path to success, in which she would continue to publish somewhat quiet, yet highly skilled and
accomplished poems.

In 1963, after eight years of literary silence, Rich surprised
her audience by breaking away from the style of her earlier
work with the publication of *Snapshots of a Daughter-in-Law*.
The more personal tone and the looser forms liberated Rich;
except for a brief pause with *Necessities of Life*, she would
never again write the neat, traditional poems that she had
penned in her twenties. As politics became an inseparable
part of her life, the style and subjects of her poetry changed
dramatically.

In the late 1960s, Rich's poetry became more radical and

revolutionary, infusing verse with politics; with the publication of *Leaflets,* several critics commented on the negative direction in which Rich's poetry was headed. Critic Robert Boyers wrote, "The problem is that progressively she falls prey to ideological fashions like the will to change, so that, though she is too intelligent ever to mouth petty slogans, she allows herself to be

National Medal for the Arts

In July, 1997, sixty-eight-year-old Adrienne Rich caused a controversy when she refused the National Medal for the Arts. Seven days before the House would vote to end the National Endowment for the Arts, Rich received a call from the White House inviting her to a ceremony in which she and eleven others would be presented with the National Medal for the Arts. Rich surprised the White House when she refused: "I cannot accept such an award from President Clinton or this White House because the very meaning of art, as I understand it, is incompatible with the cynical politics of this administration."

Rich wrote a letter to explain her refusal to Jane Alexander, the head of the NEA, that was published in the *New York Times.* "The radical disparities of wealth and power in America are widening at a devastating rate," she wrote. "A President cannot meaningfully honor certain token artists while the people at large are so dishonored." Rich insisted her refusal was not about a single individual (President Clinton), but about the larger issues of injustice. She felt that as a poet and essayist, she was committed to the public. She concluded her letter to Alexander with a hope for the future: "In the end, I don't think we can separate art from overall human dignity and hope. My concern for my country is inextricable from my concerns as an artist. I could not participate in a ritual which would feel so hypocritical to me."

violated by them" (Cooper 156). To him the book was clearly "a decline in the poet's career" (155). However, for the most part, Rich continued to impress critics; she received positive reviews, and her book, *Diving into the Wreck,* won the National Book Award.

It was not until Rich became deeply involved in the Women's Liberation Movement and began openly identifying as a radical lesbian-feminist that the critics became noticeably divisive in their readings of her work. "The nature of Rich's critical reception, too, underwent a transformation, and the detached attitude of many critics gave way to either unconditional enthusiasm or categorical rejection," claims Sylvia Henneberg in her article "The Self-Categorization, Self-Canonization, and Self-Periodization of Adrienne Rich" (Henneberg 270). Whereas many feminists upheld Rich's work as brilliant, without ever looking beyond the political themes, others in the literary community abruptly rejected her poems and prose as propaganda.

Of Woman Born certainly received the most scathing criticism of all of her work, with many reviews rippling with blatant homophobia and sexism. In the late seventies and eighties, America was beginning the battle of the culture wars, and Rich was, much by choice, right in the midst of the uproar. Her nonfiction was in general more political and incendiary than her poetry; audiences often seemed, in their reactions, unable to separate one from the other. However, it is also likely that Rich, through her interviews and outspoken views, encouraged her readers to become familiar with her politics when they read her poetry. All of this resulted in a criticism of her work that tended to be influenced by political alliances rather than poetics.

The reactions to *Of Woman Born* especially exemplify how Rich's more radical prose has shaped the way she is often read and perceived as a poet. From the seventies on, Rich was labeled a political poet, or in Alicia Ostriker's words, "a poet of ideas." These descriptions earned her devoted respect from some readers and caustic criticism from others. "Channeling most of our comments on [Rich's] poetry through her prose, we have tended to focus our attention on the poet's radical prose voice of the seventies and eighties, generating a one-sided image of her poetry which, despite all efforts, ultimately fails to reflect the complexity and changeability of her poetry," observes Henneberg (Henneberg 268). Many readers interested in feminist politics saw Rich as the most significant poet of the twentieth century; those who felt offended or excluded by her work simply dismissed her poetry as polemical or hysterical.

Much of the early criticism was painful for Rich; however, with age, she has been able to brush off most of the censures and claims that the negative criticism "bothers me a lot less now" (Rothschild). She recognizes that it is rare for critics to focus on her work alone: "It's not just about me and my work. It's about movements of which I am a part. It's about a whole social structure that is threatened or feeling itself threatened" (Rothschild). Yet, at the same time, Rich has often pointed out that it is also impossible for her to separate her work from her political convictions.

Rich's work has also influenced the Women's Movement, and, in celebrating and examining the meaning of a lesbian identity, her theories have also been a source of debate among feminists. During the eighties and nineties, feminist scholars challenged the limiting identity politics of the seventies, and several feminists criticized Rich for placing too much emphasis on woman-identification as the basis for lesbian identity. Critics also reproached her for her apparent anti-sexual position: her definition of "lesbianism" basically excluded sexuality. For example, at a feminist conference at Barnard College in 1982, the feminist historian Alice Echols accused Rich "of taking the sex out of lesbianism by championing women's sexuality as more diffuse and spiritual than the sexuality of men" (Brownmiller 315). Since then, Rich has revised some of her earlier views on lesbian identity and sexuality; yet it is important to note that when she wrote "Compulsory Heterosexuality," her groundbreaking ideas incited feminists to reconsider and debate the meanings of heterosexuality and lesbianism.

In the seventies, Rich directed her work toward a lesbian-feminist audience but she always kept one foot in the literary community. Even when she was involved in small "marginalized" journals, contributing much of her work to these feminist presses, all of her books were published with W.W. Norton, one of the most prestigious commercial publishing houses in the country. In 1977, she told Elly Bulkin she was in conflict about publishing with Norton: "It happens to be incredibly sexist—about as patriarchal as you can get ... I feel strongly that the women's presses and the women's media are a lifeline that have to be supported. They are making possible the art and ideas of the future. But making the move to a woman's press is something I have yet to do. For a variety of reasons—one being that I want my books to be distributed, to be available as widely as possible" (Bulkin 60). Rich continues to publish with Norton. Even with her more radical work, Rich has managed to straddle both the margins and the mainstream, an accomplishment that has contributed to her popularity.

Rich's style and subject matter have undergone significant changes since 1951, and she is one of the first to admit this. She distrusts the universal and believes that strength is found in the flux, in the constant changing of her work. In the eighties and nineties, she rejuvenated the lost American tradition of political poetry with poems written in the long, passionate style of Walt Whitman. In more recent poetry, Rich challenges her readers to think beyond the present or local, to participate in more global experiences.

In his foreword to her first book, written over fifty years ago, W.H. Auden praised Rich for her manners and modesty: "Miss Rich, who is, I understand, twenty-one years old, displays a modesty not so common at that age, which disclaims any extraordinary vision, and a love for her medium, a determination to ensure that whatever she writes shall, at least, not be shoddily made" (*Adrienne Rich's Poetry and Prose* 278). Auden commended Rich for knowing her place in the tradition of poetry, and he sensed that Rich was not ready to break out on her own: "Radical changes and significant novelty in artistic style can only occur when there has been a radical change in human sensibility to require them," he prophetically claimed.

In a sense, Auden's statement has become the cornerstone of Rich's career: as her life has undergone major transformations, so has her poetry. Rich's poems have changed so dramatically since her first book, *A Change of World*, that it is unlikely that Auden, if he were alive today, would even recognize her work. As Rich's poetry has changed and evolved, her critics have also had to re-examine their perspectives and readings of her work. Despite the controversy that often surrounds Rich's name, it is clear that she has impacted American literature, as well as the rights of women, in lasting and meaningful ways.

eleven

Lasting Impressions

I happen to think [poetry] makes a huge difference. Other people's poetry has made a huge difference in my life. It has changed the way I saw the world. It has changed the way I felt about the world. It has changed the way I have understood another human being.

—Adrienne Rich, in an interview
with Matthew Rothschild

ADRIENNE RICH IS ONE OF THE major poets of the last half of the twentieth century. She has published more than sixteen volumes of poetry, four books of nonfiction, and has been the recipient of major literary awards, including the National Book Award, the Fellowship of the Academy of American Poets, the Ruth Lilly Poetry Prize, the Dorothea Tanning Prize for mastery in the art of poetry given by the Academy of American Poets, the MacArthur "genius" grant, and the Bollingen Prize. Rich's poems have been anthologized in over sixty collections, and the only Norton Critical Edition that concentrates on the works of a living poet is *Adrienne Rich's Poetry*, published in 1975. Today she is probably the most popular literary poet, reaching far larger audiences than most other critically acclaimed poets. She is also one of the country's most eloquent and provocative voices on the politics of race, sexuality, women's rights, power, and language.

Rich's poetry changed significantly in the sixties, when she became involved in fighting for civil rights and protesting the war in Vietnam, and then again in the seventies, when she joined the Women's Movement and then came out as a lesbian Not only has Rich left lasting impressions on American poetry, she has also influenced thousands of women and helped raise women's status in academia and in general. Her work has had a tremendous impact on women's studies and her ideas prompted a reexamination of literature, language, and history from women's perspectives. Her essays have contributed to the development of feminist and queer theory, and challenged various institutions, including compulsory heterosexuality, patriarchal motherhood, and the exploitation of capitalism.

Rich has also touched many personal lives through her work. For example, the lesbian writer Blanche Boyd recalls first encountering Rich's poetry in the late sixties in a graduate school seminar:

Nothing I was being taught could account for the enormous impact Rich's poetry had upon me. Her technical virtuosity was extraordinary, but it was not simply technique that (for instance) left me in tears in the cafeteria ... In Rich's work I found Sylvia Plath's rage without the self-destructiveness; I found an intelligence as delicate and dispassionate as a razor ... The release I felt reading her was tremendous. She functioned for me as a kind of spiritual chronicler, venting feelings I didn't know I had. (Boyd 9)

As an "out" lesbian poet, Rich helped lesbian writers Minnie Bruce Pratt and Marilyn Hacker, as well as many younger gay and lesbian poets around the world to publish their work. Her frank discussion and celebration of lesbian sexuality have contributed to a more open discussion of homosexuality today in academia, politics, and popular culture.

Although Rich is best known for feminist and lesbian politics, she is one of most powerful voices of our time speaking out for justice. A visionary poet, Rich's poems suggest other possibilities, other ways of living. She wants people to realize that they are not trapped in the present, that they can change the course of history. "We are not simply trapped in the present ... We do have choices. We're living through a certain part of history that needs us to live it and make it and write it," she once said, and this is a principle she has lived by (*Arts of the Possible* 166). She despises complacency and the devaluing of poetry in this country. Still, at seventy-five, she maintains hope that poetry will play a part in revolutionizing the world. Although she is now more welcoming of the participation of men than she was in the seventies, she still believes that women must lead this revolution. "I still believe very strongly that there isn't going to be any kind of movement joined, any mass movement, that does not involve leadership by woman," she explained to

Rothschild. "This is the only way that I see major change approaching."

On a personal level, Rich is well acquainted with suffering.

Best American Poetry

In 1996 Adrienne Rich was asked to edit the *Best American Poetry* series, and although she was dubious of the series' intentions, she agreed as long as she was given complete editorial control. After reading through both well known and smaller journals, she chose a rich variety of poems for the anthology. The series editor, David Lehman, wrote in the introduction, "More African-American, Native American, Asian-American, Latino, and gay and lesbian poets are represented here than ever before, and their pieces weave a lush and exquisite tapestry of thought and feeling."

A year later, Lehman invited the critic Harold Bloom to edit *The Best of the Best American Poetry 1988–1997* by selecting seventy-five poems from the 750 contained in the series' first ten volumes. In an obvious rejection of Rich's politics, Bloom did not include any poems from the 1996 edition. Without naming her specifically, Bloom likely included Rich among those "enemies of the aesthetic who are in the act of overwhelming us." He accused Rich of choosing poems based only on "the race, gender, sexual orientation, ethnic origin and political purpose of the would-be poet."

Rich, however, stood by her decision, explaining her criteria in an article in *The Nation*. She was looking for "nongeneric voices," "poems with a core," poems that were "durable and daring," and poetry "that was redemptive." Rich also pointed out that the literary world needed to be more open to marginalized voices; the majority of poets published in literary magazines were white, and the majority of awards were administered by white judges and bestowed upon white men, a practice Rich called "literary apartheid."

She has battled physical ailments and intense emotional losses. Throughout her life she has struggled with feelings of isolation or separation, and poetry has helped her to find her way through difficult times.

> But however isolated or unheard you may feel, if you have the need to write poetry, are compelled to write it, you go on, whether there is resonance or not. You have to give your art everything you can—I don't mean only writing, but studying other poets and poetics, thinking, reading what poets have written other than their poetry. Thinking about the place of poetry in the world, what might be possible. What your place as a poet might be. You have to do that. (da Costa)

Rich not only deeply influenced her own generation with her politics and poetry, but she has also made a strong impression on younger people. Many students, activists, poets, gay men, and lesbians have turned to Rich's work for inspiration and solace. She has been both poet and role model for people searching for an alternative to that mainstream culture.

For the gay and lesbian community, in particular, Rich has been an inspiration from the beginning. Since 1975, she has lived her life openly and honestly as a lesbian. She is certainly one of the most widely read lesbian poets in America. Her prose and poetry have celebrated lesbian identity and love, and exposed the violence of homophobia and the powerlessness of silence. When asked about the costs of speaking honestly about homophobia in her poems, in terms of critics and her career, Rich quickly responded, "What would be the cost of *not* doing it?" (*Adrienne Rich's Poetry and Prose* 271).

Rich adamantly believes that the poet does not belong in an ivory tower, but should act as an eyewitness to the world:

"Writers and intellectuals can name, we can describe, we can depict, we can witness—without sacrificing craft, nuance, or beauty. Above all, and at our best, we may sometimes help question the questions" (*Arts of the Possible* 167). Despite the impact of her political activism, her lectures, her ground-breaking essays and theory, Rich has always considered herself first and foremost a poet. "I intend to go on making poetry," she told Moyers. "I think that there is a real culture of resistance here—of artists' and of other kinds of voices—that will continue, however bad things get in this country. I want to make myself a part of that and do my work as well as I can. I want to love those I love as well as I can, and I want to love life as well as I can" (Moyers 350).

Spanning a distinguished fifty-year career, Rich has explored sexuality, racism, history, gender, and language with perseverance and courage. Her transformation over the years, as poet and as a citizen of the world, has been astonishing and inspiring. She is a poet who has touched the lives of many, and as long as she is still able to write, and as long there is injustice, Adrienne Rich will continue, through her poetry and prose, to contribute to making the world a better place. When Matthew Rothschild asked Rich if she ever got tired of writing about racism, homophobia, misogyny, she replied, "No, I'm not tired of the issues; I'm tired of the lists—the litany ... How can I be tired of the issues? The issues are our lives."

WORKS CITED

Bennett, Paula. *My Life as a Loaded Gun: Dickinson, Plath, Rich, and Female Creativity.* Urbana, IL: University of Illinois Press, 1990.

Bere, Carol. "The Road Taken: Adrienne Rich in the 1990s." *The Literary Review* 43, no. 4 (Summer 2000): 550–60.

Boland, Eavan. "Conversation with Adrienne Rich." 4 pages. Lannan Foundation. (26 August 2004). <*http://www.lannan.org/video/catalog/vid_PQR.htm*>.

Boyd, Blanche M. "Adrienne Rich Interview." *Christopher Street:* 1, no. 7 (January 1977): 9–16.

Bulkin, Elly and Joan Larkin, eds. *Amazon Poetry.* Brooklyn: Out & Out Books, 1975.

Bulkin, Elly. "An Interview with Adrienne Rich: Part I." *Conditions:* 1, no. 1. (April 1977): 50–65.

———. "An Interview with Adrienne Rich: Part II." *Conditions:* 1, no. 2. (October 1977): 53–66.

Brownmiller, Susan. *In Our Time: Memoir of A Revolution.* New York: Dial Press, 1999.

Cooper, Jane Roberta, ed. *Reading Adrienne Rich: Reviews and Re-Visions, 1951–81.* Ann Arbor: The University of Michigan Press, 1984.

da Costa, Paulo. "Interview with Adrienne Rich." *Samsära Quarterly,* 2001. 2 pages. Modern American Poetry (26 August 2004). <*http://www.english.uiuc.edu/maps/poets/m_r/rich/onlineints.htm*>.

Faderman, Lillian. *Odd Girls and Twilight Lovers.* New York: Penguin Books, 1991.

Henneberg, Sylvia. "The Self-Categorization, Self-Canonization, and Self-Periodization of Adrienne Rich," in *Challenging Boundaries: Gender & Periodization.* Eds. Margaret Dickie and Joyce Warren. Athens: University of Georgia Press, (2000). 267–83

Kalstone, David. *Five Temperaments.* New York: Oxford University Press, 1977.

Klein, Michael. "A Rich Life: Adrienne Rich on Poetry, Politics, and Personal Revelation." *Boston Phoenix,* June 1999. 3 pages. Modern American Poetry (26 August 2004).

<*http://www.english.uiuc.edu/maps/poets/m_r/rich/onlineints.htm*>.

Langdell, Cheri Colby. *Adrienne Rich: The Moment of Change.* Contributions in Women's Studies, Number 198. Westport, Conn: Praeger, 2004.

Martin, Wendy. *An American Triptych: Anne Bradstreet, Emily Dickinson, Adrienne Rich.* Chapel Hill: The University of North Carolina Press, 1984.

Montenegro, David. "Adrienne Rich: An Interview with David Montenegro." *Adrienne Rich's Poetry and Prose* 258–272

Moyers, Bill. *The Language of Life: A Festival of Poets.* New York: Doubleday, 1995.

Nelson, Cary. Modern American Poetry (26 August 2004). <*http://www.english.uiuc.edu/maps/poets/m_r/rich/onlineints.htm*>.

O'Mahoney, John. "Poet and Pioneer." *The Guardian*, 15 June 2002. 5 pages. Guardian Unlimited. (20 August 2004). <*http://books. guardian.co.uk/review/story/0%2C12084%2C737290%2C00.html*>.

Plath, Sylvia. *The Unabridged Journals of Sylvia Plath.* Ed. Karen V. Kukil. New York: Anchor Books, 2000. 368.

Rich, Adrienne. *Adrienne Rich's Poetry.* Barbara Charlesworth Gelpi and Albert Gelpi, eds. New York: W.W. Norton & Company, 1975.

———. *Adrienne Rich's Poetry and Prose.* Barbara Charlesworth Gelpi and Albert Gelpi, eds. New York: W.W. Norton & Company, 1993.

———. *Arts of the Possible.* New York: W.W. Norton & Company, 2001.

———. *An Atlas of the Difficult World: Poems 1988–1991.* New York: W.W. Norton & Company, 1991.

———. *Blood, Bread, and Poetry.* New York: W.W. Norton & Company, 1986.

———. *Collected Early Poems,* 1950–1970. New York: Norton, 1993.

———. *The Dream of a Common Language: Poems 1974–1977.* New York: W.W. Norton & Company, 1978.

———. *Leaflets: Poems 1965–1968.* New York: W.W. Norton & Company, 1969.

———. *Of Woman Born: Motherhood as Experience and Institution.* New York: W.W. Norton & Company, 1976.

———. *On Lies, Secrets, and Silence, Selected Prose 1966–1978.* New York: W.W. Norton & Company, 1979.

———. *Snapshots of a Daughter-in-Law.* New York: W.W. Norton & Company, 1956.

———. *What Is Found There: Notebooks on Poetry and Politics.* New York: W.W. Norton & Company, 1993.

———. "Why I Refused the National Medal for the Arts." *Los Angeles Times Book Section,* 3 August 1997. 4 pages. Modern American Poetry. (20 August 2004). *<http://www.english.uiuc.edu/maps/poets/m_r/rich/onlineessays.htm>.*

———. *Your Native Land, Your Life.* New York: W.W. Norton & Company, 1986.

Rosen, Ruth. *The World Split Open.* New York: Penguin Books, 2000.

Rothschild, Matthew. "Adrienne Rich." *The Progressive* January 1994. 8 pages. Modern American Poetry. (20 August 2004). *<http://www.english.uiuc.edu/maps/poets/m_r/rich/progressive.htm>.*

Yorke, Liz. *Adrienne Rich: Passion, Politics, and the Body.* London: SAGE Publications, 1997.

1929	Adrienne Rich is born May 16, in Baltimore, Maryland, to Arnold and Helen Jones Rich. She is home schooled until age nine.
1951	Graduates from Radcliffe College. Her first book, *A Change of World*, is chosen by W.H. Auden for the Yale Younger Poets Competition.
1952–53	Wins Guggenheim Fellowship to travel in Europe and England. Onset of rheumatoid arthritis.
1953	Marries Alfred H. Conrad, an economist teaching at Harvard.
1955	Birth of son David Conrad. Publishes *The Diamond Cutters and Other Poems*. Awarded the Ridgley Torrence Memorial Award of the Poetry Society of America.
1957	Birth of Paul Conrad.
1959	Birth of Jacob Conrad.
1960	Wins National Institute of Arts and Letters Award for poetry.
1962–63	Wins Amy Lowell Traveling Fellowship. Becomes member of the Academy of American Poets.
1963	Publishes *Snapshots of a Daughter-in-Law: Poems 1954–1962*. Wins Bess Hokin Prize of *Poetry Magazine*.
1966	*Necessities of Life: Poems 1962–1965* published. Moves with family to New York City. Politically active in Civil Rights Movement, protests against the Vietnam War.
1967	*Selected Poems* published in England. Honorary doctorate from Wheaton College. Undergoes orthopedic surgery for arthritis.
1967–69	Lecturer, Swarthmore College. Adjunct Professor, Writing Division, Columbia University School of Arts.
1968	Begins teaching in SEEK program at City College of New York and continues 1968–72, and 1974–1975. Wins Eunice Tietjens Memorial Prize of *Poetry Magazine*. Her father Arnold Richard dies after battling a long illness.

1969	*Leaflets: Poems 1965–1968* published.
1970	Death of husband Alfred Conrad.
1971	Publishes *The Will to Change: Poems 1968–1970*. Wins Shelley Memorial Award of The Poetry Society of America. Becomes increasingly active with the Women's Liberation Movement.
1972–73	Appointed Hurst Visiting Professor of Creative Writing, Brandeis University.
1973	*Diving into the Wreck: Poems 1971–1973* published.
1974	Appointed Professor of English, City College of New York. *Diving into the Wreck* wins the National Book Award, but Rich declines to accept it individually. Shares the award with two other nominated poets, Audre Lorde and Alice Walker. Accept the award together on behalf of all women.
1975	*Adrienne Rich's Poetry*, edited by Barbara Charlesworth Gelpi and Albert Gelpi (Norton Critical Edition), published. *Poems: Selected and New, 1950–1974* published. Awarded Lucy Martin Donnelley Fellow of Bryn Mawr College.
1976	Publishes nonfiction book, *Of Woman Born: Motherhood as Experience and Institution*. Publishes *Twenty-One Love Poems*. Begins lifelong partnership with Michelle Cliff. Delivers speech "It is the Lesbian in Us" at a conference of the Modern Language Association.
1976–79	Professor of English, Douglass College, Rutgers University.
1980	Undergoes orthopedic surgery for arthritis.
1981	Publishes *A Wild Patience Has Taken Me This Far: Poems 1978–1981*. Awarded Fund for Human Dignity Award, National Gay Task Force.
1981–83	Co-edits *Sinister Wisdom*, a lesbian/feminist journal, with partner Michelle Cliff.

1981–87	Appointed A.D. White Professor-at-Large, Cornell University.
1982	Undergoes orthopedic surgery for arthritis.
1983	Publishes *Sources*.
1983–84	Appointed Visiting Professor, Scripps College, Claremont, California.
1984	*The Fact of a Doorframe: Poems Selected and New 1950–1984* published. Moves to Santa Cruz, California with Cliff.
1984–86	Appointed Distinguished Visiting Professor, San Jose State University.
1986	Publishes *Your Native Land, Your Life: Poems*, and a book of nonfiction, *Blood, Bread and Poetry: Selected Prose 1979–1985*. Awarded Ruth Lilly Poetry Prize. Tenth Anniversary Edition *Of Woman Born* published.
1986–93	Appointed Professor of English, Stanford University.
1987	Awarded honorary doctorate, College of Wooster, Ohio, honorary doctorate, Brandeis University, and Brandeis Creative Arts Medal in Poetry.
1989	Publishes *Time's Power: Poems 1985–1988*. Appointed Marjorie Kovler Fellow, University of Chicago. Wins National Poetry Association Award for Distinguished Service to the Art of Poetry and the Elmer Holmes Bobst Award in Arts and Letters, New York University.
1990	Awarded honorary doctorate, City College of New York and Harvard University. Wins Bay Area Book Reviewers Award in Poetry. Becomes member of Department of Literature, American Academy and Institute of Arts and Letters. Becomes member of the founding editorial group of *Bridges: A Journal for Jewish Feminists and Our Friends*.
1991	Publishes *An Atlas of the Difficult World: Poems 1988–1991*. Wins the Commonwealth Award in Literature.

1991–1992	Wins honorary doctorate, Swarthmore College. Wins Robert Frost Silver Medal of the Poetry Society of America and the William Whitehead Award of the Publishing Triangle for lifetime achievement in letters. *An Atlas of the Difficult World* receives the *Los Angeles Times* Book Award in Poetry and the Lenore Marshall/Nation Award. Julia Arden Conrad, and Charles Reddington Conrad grandchildren, are born.
1992	Undergoes spinal surgery.
1993	Publishes *Collected Early Poems, 1950–1970* and *What is Found There: Notebooks on Poetry and Politics. An Atlas of the Difficult World* awarded Poet's Prize.
1994	Wins MacArthur "Genius Grant" Fellowship.
1995	Publishes *Dark Fields of the Republic: Poems 1991–1995*, wins Lammy Award for Lesbian Poetry.
1996	Edits controversial *The Best American Poetry, 1996*. Awarded Tanning Prize for Mastery of Poetry by Academy of American Poets. Appointed a Chancellor of the Academy of American Poets.
1997	Wins the National Medal for the Arts, but declines it, protesting against the vote in House of Representatives to end the National Endowment for the Arts and other policies of the Clinton administration regarding the arts.
1999	Publishes *Midnight Salvage: Poems 1995–1998*.
2001	Publishes *The Art of The Possible and Fox: Poems 1998–2000*.
2002	Participates in many antiwar activities, protests against the war in Iraq. Appointed a chancellor of the Academy of American Poets.
2003	Winner of the 2003 Yale Bollingen Prize for American Poetry. Participates in the National Day of Poetry against the War.
2004	Publishes *The School Among the Ruins: Poems 2000–2004*.

WORKS BY ADRIENNE RICH

POETRY

A Change of World (1951)

The Diamond Cutters and Other Poems (1955)

Snapshots of a Daughter-in-Law: Poems 1954–1962 (1963)

Necessities of Life: Poems 1962–1965 (1966)

Selected Poems (1967)

Leaflets: Poems 1965–1968 (1969)

The Will to Change: Poems 1968–1970 (1971)

Diving into the Wreck: Poems 1971–1972 (1973)

Poems: Selected and New, 1950–1975 (1975)

Twenty-One Love Poems (1976)

The Dream of a Common Language: Poems 1974–1977 (1978)

A Wild Patience Has Taken Me This Far: Poems 1978–1981 (1981)

Sources (1983)

The Fact of a Doorframe: Poems Selected and New 1950–1984 (1984)

Your Native Land, Your Life: Poems (1986)

Time's Power: Poems 1985–1988 (1989)

An Atlas of the Difficult World: Poems 1988–1991 (1991)

Collected Early Poems 1950–1970 (1993)

Dark Fields of the Republic: Poems 1991–1995 (1995)

Midnight Salvage: Poems 1995–1998 (1999)

Fox: Poems 1998–2000 (2001)

The School Among the Ruins: Poems 2000–2004 (2004)

PROSE

Of Woman Born: Motherhood as Experience and Institution (1976)

On Lies, Secrets, and Silence: Selected Prose, 1966–1978 (1979)

Blood, Bread, and Poetry: Selected Prose, 1979–1985 (1986)

What is Found There: Notebooks on Poetry and Politics (1993)

Arts of the Possible: Essays and Conversations (2001)

FURTHER READING

Bennett, Paula. *My Life as a Loaded Gun: Dickinson, Plath, Rich, and Female Creativity.* Urbana, IL: University of Illinois Press, 1990.

Birkle, Carmen. *Women's Stories of the Looking Glass: Autobiographical Reflections and Self-Representations in the Poetry of Sylvia Plath, Adrienne Rich, and Audre Lorde.* American Studies, A Monograph Series. Vol. 72. Munich: Wilhelm Fink, 1996.

Caris, Jane. "Body as Metaphor in the Poetry of Adrienne Rich." *Pleiades* 16.2 (Spring 1996): 105–115.

Cooper, Jane R. ed. *Reading Adrienne Rich: Reviews and Re-visions, 1951–81.* Ann Arbor: University of Michigan Press, 1984.

Eagleton, Mary. "Adrienne Rich, Location and the Body." *Journal of Gender Studies* 9, no. 3. (November 2000): 299–312.

Erickson, Peter. "Singing America: From Walt Whitman to Adrienne Rich." *Kenyon Review* 17, no.1 (Winter 1995): 103–19.

Estrin, Barbara L. "Space-Off and Voice-Over: Adrienne Rich and Wallace Stevens." *Women's Studies* 25, no.1 (Nov 1995): 23–46.

Flowers, Betty S. "Wrestling with the Mother and the Father: 'His' and 'Her' in Adrienne Rich." *Private Voices, Public Lives: Women Speak on the Literary Life.* Ed. Nancy O. Nelson. Denton: University of North Texas Press, 1995. 54–63.

Gelpi, Albert. Introduction. *"A Whole New Poetry Beginning Here"*: Adrienne Rich in the Eighties and Nineties, ed. Albert Gelpi and Jacqueline Vaught Brogan. Special issue devoted exclusively to Adrienne Rich. *Women's Studies* 27, no. 4 (June 1998): 309–310.

Greenwald, Elissa. "The Dream of a Common Language: Vietnam Poetry as Reformation of Language and Feeling in the Poems of Adrienne Rich." *Journal of American Culture* 16, no. 3 (Fall 1993): 97–102.

Henneberg, Sylvia. "The Self-Categorization, Self-Canonization, and Self-Periodization of Adrienne Rich." *Challenging Boundaries: Gender and Periodization.* Eds. Joyce W. Warren and Margaret Dickie. Athens, Georgia: The University of Georgia Press. 2000.

———. "The 'Slow Turn of Consciousness': Adrienne Rich's Family Plot." *Women's Studies* 27, no. 4 (June 1998): 347–58.

Herzog, Anne. "Adrienne Rich and the Discourse of Decolonization." *Centennial Review* 33, no. 3 (Summer 1989): 258–277.

Keyes, Claire. *The Aesthetics of Power: the Poetry of Adrienne Rich.* Athens: University of Georgia Press, 1986.

Klein, Karen W. "Adrienne Rich: 'Stuck to Earth.' " *Daughters of Valor: Contemporary Jewish American Women Writers.* Eds. Jay L. Halio and Ben Siegel. Newark, DE: University of Delaware Press, 1997: 194–208.

Langdell, Cheri Colby. *Adrienne Rich: The Moment of Change.* Contributions in Women's Studies, Number 198. Westport, Conn: Praeger, 2004.

Martin, Wendy. *An American Triptych: Anne Bradstreet, Emily Dickinson, Adrienne Rich.* Chapel Hill: University of North Carolina Press, 1984.

Matson, Suzanne. "Talking to Our Father: The Political and Mythical Appropriations of Adrienne Rich and Sharon Olds." *American Poetry Review* 18, no.6 (Nov.–Dec. 1989): 35–41.

McGuirk, Kevin. "Philoctetes Radicalized: 'Twenty-One Love Poems' and the Lyric Career of Adrienne Rich." *Contemporary Literature* 34, no.1 (Spring 1993): 61–87.

Ratcliffe, Krista. *Anglo-American Feminist Challenges to the Rhetorical Traditions: Virginia Woolf, Mary Daly, Adrienne Rich.* Carbondale: Southern Illinois University Press, 1996.

Rich, Adrienne, ed. *The Best American Poetry 1996.* New York: Scribners, 1996.

Rich, Adrienne. *Adrienne Rich's Poetry.* Barbara Charlesworth Gelpi and Albert Gelpi, eds. New York: W.W. Norton & Company, 1975.

————. *Adrienne Rich's Poetry and Prose.* Barbara Charlesworth Gelpi and Albert Gelpi, eds. New York: W.W. Norton & Company, 1993.

Slowick, Mary. "The Friction of the Mind: The Early Poetry of Adrienne Rich." *Massachusetts Review* 25, no. 1 (Spring 1984): 142–160.

Spender, Dale. *Women of Ideas and What Men Have Done to Them: from Aphra Behn to Adrienne Rich.* Boston: Routledge & Kegan Paul, 1982.

Stein, Kevin. *Private Poets, Worldly Acts.* Athens: Ohio University Press, 1996.

Stimpson, Catharine. "Adrienne Rich and Lesbian/Feminist Poetry." *Parnassus* 12–13, no. 2–1 (Spring–Winter 1985): 249–268.

Templeton, Alice. *The Dream and the Dialogue: Adrienne Rich's Feminist Poetics.* Knoxville: The University of Tennessee Press, 1994.

Vendler, Helen. "Mapping the Air - Adrienne Rich and Jorie Graham." *Soul Says: On Recent Poetry.* Cambridge: The Belknap Press of Harvard University Press, 1995: 212–234.

Walker, Jeffrey A. "Remapping Freudian America: Adrienne Rich and the Adult Son." *North Dakota Quarterly* 62, no. 3 (Summer 1994–95): 76–93.

Werner, Craig H. *Adrienne Rich: the Poet and her Critics.* Chicago: American Library Association, 1988.

Yorke, Liz. *Adrienne Rich: Passion, Politics, and the Body.* London: SAGE Publications, 1997.

Zimmerman, Lee. "An Eye for an I: Emerson and Some 'True' Poems of Robinson Jeffers, William Everson, Robert Penn Warren, and Adrienne Rich." *Contemporary Literature* 33, no.4 (Winter 1992): 645–64.

WEBSITES:

Adrienne Rich Station
www.adriennerich.hpg.ig.com.br/resources.htm

American Literature on the Web
www.nagasaki-gaigo.ac.jp/ishikawa/amlit/r/rich21.htm

Modern American Poetry
www.english.uiuc.edu/maps/poets/m_r/rich/rich.htm

Norton Poets Online
www.nortonpoets.com/richa.htm

PAL: Perspectives in American Literature
www.csustan.edu/english/reuben/pal/chap10/rich.html

INDEX

CONTRIBUTORS

AMY SICKELS is a freelance writer living in New York City. She received her MFA in creative writing from Penn State University and she has published short stories, essays, and book reviews in numerous journals, including *Fourth Genre*, *Kalliope*, and *Literary Review*.

LESLÉA NEWMAN is the author of 50 books including the picture books *Heather Has Two Mommies* and *The Boy Who Cried Fabulous*; the short story collections *A Letter to Harvey Milk* and *Out of the Closet and Nothing to Wear*; the poetry collection *Still Life with Buddy*; the novels *In Every Laugh a Tear* and *Jailbait*; and the writing manual, *Write from the Heart*. She has received many literary awards including Poetry Fellowships from the Massachusetts Artists Fellowship Foundation and the National Endowment for the Arts, the Highlights for Children Fiction Writing Award, the James Baldwin Award for Cultural Achievement, and three Pushcart Prize Nominations. Nine of her books have been Lambda Literary Award finalists.